ASIA

PACIFIC OCEAN

CHINA

IA

Nanking.   .Chusan   JAPAN
Chingtechen.   I.

                Amoy   FORMOSA
alcutta.   Canton
          Macao.
                          PHILIPPINE
                          ISLANDS   To Mexico

                        CHINA
                        SEA

                MALAYA
                  STRAIT OF
                  MALACCA

                          SPICE ISLANDS
                              OR
                          MOLUCCAS

                    EAST INDIES

STRAITS OF SUNDA

INDIAN   *Principal Routes of the*
                                                Porcelain Trade
OCEAN   *between*
                                                China and Europe

              AUSTRALIA   XVIII – EARLY XIX CENTURIES

                                                            NEW ZEALAND

CHINA-TRADE PORCELAIN

FRONTISPIECE

Cup and saucer showing Western merchants in a chinaware shop in Canton. Continental market
1725–1740

CHINA-
TRADE
PORCELAIN

An Account of Its Historical Background,

Manufacture, and Decoration and a Study of

the Helena Woolworth McCann Collection.

Published for the Winfield Foundation

and the Metropolitan Museum of Art

JOHN GOLDSMITH PHILLIPS

Harvard University Press
Cambridge, Massachusetts 1956

Printed in England by W. S. Cowell Ltd, Butter Market, Ipswich
Designed by Peter Oldenburg
Library of Congress catalog card no. 56–11749

The Helena Woolworth McCann collection of China-Trade porcelain is a lasting tribute to the knowledge and judgment of the collector whose name it bears. The collection consists of about 4,000 pieces, including a number of large tea and dinner services, made in China to the order of European and American clients during the seventeenth, eighteenth, and nineteenth centuries. Assembling such a comprehensive and distinguished group not only called for rare insight and informed taste, but required extensive travel and search in Europe.

During the formation of her collection Mrs. McCann was in close touch with Henry Francis duPont of Winterthur, Delaware, who was bringing together his own remarkable collection of China-Trade porcelain, principally pieces made for the American and English markets. While in Europe she enjoyed the cordial friendship of another outstanding collector, the late Ricardo R. Espirito Santo Silva of Lisbon, which proved most helpful in her studies of the porcelains made for Continental markets. It is noteworthy that all three of these collections have been made available to the public.

Following Mrs. McCann's untimely death in 1938 her children, Mrs. Richard Charlton, Mrs. Joseph V. McMullan, and Frasier W. McCann, gave her collection to the Winfield Foundation, created in her memory for educational and charitable purposes. To make this material available to the American public as a source of pleasure and instruction, in 1942 the Foundation lent half the porcelains to the Museum of Fine Arts in Boston and the other half to the Metropolitan Museum of Art in New York City. Even these two great institutions could not effectively accommodate such a large and varied collection. Detailed consideration of some final disposition, made in cooperation with the officials of both these museums, was interrupted by the war. Eventually, units of the collection, varying—in quantity but not in quality—according to relative needs, were given to twenty-six museums in the United States and to one in Canada. By means of such widespread distribution this great body of material has been made accessible to students and other interested persons across the breadth of the American continent. The names and locations of the sharing institutions are listed on page vii. The Foundation is grateful for the accommodating and unquestioning spirit with which they accepted the individual allotments of porcelain arranged by John Goldsmith Phillips of the Metropolitan Museum.

Exhibitions in New York and Boston had already made the McCann collection known to many people before these gifts were made. A number of fine pieces were included in the Metropolitan Museum's historic exhibition, *The China Trade and Its Influence*, held in 1941. Two permanent galleries devoted to the display of McCann porcelains were opened in Boston's Museum of Fine Arts in 1943. That museum had received as a gift from the Winfield Foundation a carved, painted, and gilded French oak *boiserie* of the Louis XV period, removed from Sunken Orchard, Mrs. McCann's home at Oyster Bay Cove, Long Island. This fine in-

v

terior, adapted to show a quantity of the China-Trade porcelain (see Fig. 39), was set up in Boston in much the same manner as in the McCann residence. In 1946 the Metropolitan Museum arranged a special exhibition of its loan of McCann porcelain.

Each of these two special exhibitions was signalized by a separate published account. The Museum of Fine Arts issued a brochure entitled *Chinese Export Porcelain of the Helena Woolworth McCann Collection and French Paneling of the Louis XV Period,* written by the late Edwin J. Hipkiss, then the museum's distinguished Curator of Decorative Arts of Europe and America. A description of the material on view at the Metropolitan, written by the author of the present volume, appeared in the museum's *Bulletin* for February, 1946. In November, 1954 the Metropolitan opened a gallery dedicated to the permanent display of the part of the collection that had by that time been given to it.

With the dispersal of the porcelains the Trustees of the Winfield Foundation decided upon a permanent record of the original collection as a whole, one which would provide a study of the subject at large as well as a reference to the many elements of the collection that had been distributed throughout the country. The authorship of this book was entrusted to the experienced hands of John Goldsmith Phillips, Curator of Renaissance Art at the Metropolitan Museum. By special arrangement this volume is published for the Foundation by the Metropolitan Museum through the agency of the Harvard University Press.

The Foundation and its Porcelain Committee express deep appreciation to all those who have contributed to the success of this undertaking: in particular to Roland L. Redmond and Walter S. Orr, members of the Board of Directors of the Foundation, for their sage counsel; to George H. Edgell, the late Director of the Boston Museum, and his associates, Edwin J. Hipkiss, Richard B. K. McLanathan, and Mrs. Yves H. Buhler; and to Francis Henry Taylor, recent Director of the Metropolitan Museum, and his colleagues, Preston Remington, C. Louise Avery, Huldah Smith, John Goldsmith Phillips, Agnes D. Peters, Olga Krupen, and Marshall B. Davidson.

THE PORCELAIN COMMITTEE OF THE WINFIELD FOUNDATION

Joseph V. McMullan, *Chairman*
Robert L. Larner
Constance W. McMullan

DISTRIBUTION OF PORCELAINS
FROM THE McCANN COLLECTION

The number of porcelains each institution received is noted at the right.

BOSTON, MASSACHUSETTS
Museum of Fine Arts — 644

BROOKLYN, NEW YORK
Brooklyn Museum — 152

BUFFALO, NEW YORK
Albright Art Gallery — 116

CHICAGO, ILLINOIS
Art Institute of Chicago — 148

CINCINNATI, OHIO
Cincinnati Art Museum — 111

CLEVELAND, OHIO
Cleveland Museum of Art — 54

DALLAS, TEXAS
Dallas Museum of Fine Arts — 66

DETROIT, MICHIGAN
Detroit Institute of Arts — 133

FREEHOLD, NEW JERSEY
Monmouth County Historical Association — 156

GLOUCESTER, MASSACHUSETTS
Beauport — 130

HARTFORD, CONNECTICUT
Wadsworth Atheneum — 82

HOUSTON, TEXAS
Museum of Fine Arts of Houston — 80

KANSAS CITY, MISSOURI
William Rockhill Nelson Gallery of Art — 192

LOS ANGELES, CALIFORNIA
Los Angeles County Museum — 138

LOUISVILLE, KENTUCKY
J. B. Speed Art Museum — 70

MINNEAPOLIS, MINNESOTA
Minneapolis Institute of Arts — 147

NEW YORK, NEW YORK
Metropolitan Museum of Art — 441

NORFOLK, VIRGINIA
Norfolk Museum of Arts and Sciences — 63

OMAHA, NEBRASKA
Joslyn Memorial Art Museum — 57

PORTLAND, OREGON
Portland Art Museum — 163

PROVIDENCE, RHODE ISLAND
Museum of Art, Rhode Island School of Design — 70

RICHMOND, VIRGINIA
Virginia Museum of Fine Arts — 80

SAINT LOUIS, MISSOURI
City Art Museum of Saint Louis — 103

SAN FRANCISCO, CALIFORNIA
M. H. De Young Memorial Museum — 57

SPRINGFIELD, MASSACHUSETTS
Springfield Museum of Fine Arts — 169

TOLEDO, OHIO
Toledo Museum of Art — 121

TORONTO, CANADA
Royal Ontario Museum of Archaeology — 41

to Constance and Joseph McMullan

CONTENTS

PART TWO

PAGE

The McCann Collection
(*continued*)

LIST OF FIGURES

LIST OF PLATES

The Frontispiece and Plates 1–16 are from color transparencies by Anna Wachsman. The photographs for the remaining Plates are reproduced by the courtesy of the owners of the porcelains illustrated, credited in the Appendix, page 215.

FRONTISPIECE

Cup and saucer showing Western merchants in a chinaware shop in Canton. Continental market. 1725–1740

ILLUSTRATIONS IN THE APPENDIX

INTRODUCTION

The tale of China-Trade porcelain is one of sharp contrasts and vivid highlights. It is in part a Chinese story, for the ware was manufactured in China; but it is also European in that the ware was made for European—and later for American—use. It tells of those bold Westerners who first ventured to China in search of commerce, and of the Orientals who treated with them. As this story has to do with Europeans in China, it is also concerned with the influence of China upon Europe. The double imprint of East and West is the ware's distinctive hallmark.

The term China-Trade porcelain is here used to describe all those pieces made in China more or less according to Western specification and for Western use. The trade in the material was developed into a significant phase of international commerce during the eighteenth century, and it was carried on principally between China and Europe. China-Trade porcelain made for America is a phenomenon of the end of the eighteenth century and the early nineteenth century. The American trade was minor compared to that with Europe.

China-Trade porcelains are mostly tablewares. Decorative pieces, such as vases, are infrequently met with. Figure groups are very rare. Taken as a whole, the material may be divided into two general classes. There are the ordinary varieties—often made in quantity—which were either left undecorated or painted in underglaze colors; of these, the blue-and-white ware was the most popular. In addition, there are the porcelains which were executed to special order. These include both armorial china

and other porcelains with decorations painted over the glaze and based in one way or another on Western design sources. It is with this latter group that our chief interest lies, for not only does it include the most novel, interesting, and colorful of all the export porcelains, but to it belong most of the pieces in the McCann collection and in other collections of China-Trade material as well.

In this study of China-Trade porcelain as represented in the Helena Woolworth McCann collection, our aim is twofold: to review the material's strange and little-known story and to describe the collection itself.

Our account begins in China's interior, in fabulous, chimney-crested Chingtechen. Although the name of that town is unknown to all but a few foreigners, it was for centuries, as indeed it still is, China's porcelain center. There it was that the China-Trade wares were produced by the very men making the dishes, bowls, and vases for China's home market.

From Chingtechen we turn to Canton, the country's leading seaport and trading center. Canton's position in international trade is an ancient one, long antedating the arrival of the first European merchants in the sixteenth century. The annals of those early days and of the city's commercial history during the Age of Discovery and the following period of the East India Companies form a dramatic background against which our study of China-Trade porcelain may be projected. Our interest naturally centers upon the activities of the East India Companies, especially during the eighteenth century, for it was then that most of the export porcelain was sent from Chingtechen to Canton, where the finer wares received their final decorations at the hands of Cantonese painters, and all varieties were marketed and dispatched westward.

Europe had been trading in porcelain made to Western specification for almost a century before the Americans first arrived in Canton in 1784. Although the China-Trade porcelain made for America after that date was on a par with that produced for Europe, the American trade in the material, historically considered, was a minor phase of the entire porcelain commerce with the West. Hence the American aspect of the story, appropriately epitomized, is here approached in international perspective. For a more detailed account of the American trade in Chinese porcelain, together with a full description of the types of wares dispatched to the United States, the reader is referred to J. A. Lloyd Hyde's distinguished study *Oriental Lowestoft*.

At this point our story shifts from China to Europe. The use of China-Trade porcelain represents but one phase of the more general history of China's impact upon the West and of the traces left by it upon Western life and art. Since in the eyes of many Europeans porcelain was the most significant of Oriental art forms, the growth of a demand in Europe for works in this material—both for the wares imported from China and for those made after the beginning of the eighteenth century in European factories—forms an essential part of the picture. As we bring the historical section of our study to a close, we see still another result of this cultural interchange: the surprising degree to which China-Trade porcelain reflected in both form and style the ceramic art of Europe.

The final section of the book is devoted entirely to the magnificent collection of China-Trade porcelain formed by Helena Woolworth McCann. That the reader may grasp the full extent of Mrs. McCann's achievement as a collector, we present the chinaware as it appeared when the collection was intact. The location of pieces illustrated in the Plates and the distribution of the numerous services among the institutions sharing in the collection have been noted in the Appendix.

[2]

One of the curious things about the Chinese porcelain made for the Western market is that in the past it has been given many names, none of them meeting with lasting acceptance. Since the term "China-Trade porcelain" is here used for the first time as a formal designation for the ware, let us endeavor to show why at this late date a new name seems called for.

In the eighteenth-century records of the English East India Company—the powerful monopoly which controlled English trade in the Far East and handled so much of this porcelain—the material was generally described as *chinaware*. At home in England, it was known as *East India Company china*, or more simply, *East India china*. In the newly founded United States where there was no chartered company, but where from 1784 porcelain was imported from the East, the Company term used in England did not apply; like the English traders, Americans just called porcelain *chinaware*. The term *Canton china* was also used, and in both England and America, certain types of blue-and-white porcelain were known as *Nanking*, or *Nankeen*, *china* from the Chinese seaport where they were thought to have been made. The various East India Companies on the Continent each had its own name for the porcelain. The French, for example, called the pieces made for export *porcelaine de la Compagnie des Indes*.

During the nineteenth century the export of China-Trade porcelain virtually ceased. With the passage of time the origins of the pieces remaining in Europe were well-nigh forgotten, even by students of ceramic art. At length a celebrated scholar of the Victorian age William Chaffers concluded in his *Marks and Monograms* that many of the ware's most characteristic examples—that is to say, all the armorial porcelains—were manufactured in the small East Anglian town of Lowestoft, where indeed there had been a small porcelain factory. Although the facts eventually became known, Chaffers' blunder gave rise to still another name. In America, though oddly not in England or on the Continent, *Oriental Lowestoft* remains to this day the ware's popular designation.

In recent years various American scholars have attempted to lay the Lowestoft ghost. There has been a concerted effort to call the material "Chinese export porcelain." The term "China-Trade porcelain," however, is an apt, vivid, and less cumbersome designation. Apparently American and of the eighteenth century in origin, the phrase "China Trade" describes the commerce carried on in the Orient by the East India Companies and by independent merchants. The porcelains with which we are concerned form a significant part of that commerce. The words "China Trade" are therefore as truly descriptive of the porcelains as of the greater trade of which they were but a part.

[3]

In the preparation of this book I am especially indebted to Joseph V. McMullan, trustee of the Winfield Foundation, from whom at all times I have received sage and friendly council.

My colleagues in the Metropolitan Museum, C. Louise Avery and Huldah Smith, have shared their expert knowledge in the field of Western ceramics with me. J. A. Lloyd Hyde, author of *Oriental Lowestoft*, and Soame Jenyns of the British Museum are others of great knowledge and experience to whom I have profitably turned. I am also eternally in the debt of a number of scholars—chief among them Hosea Ballou Morse and Algernon Tudor-Craig—who have written on various aspects of the subject and whose works are listed in the Bibliography.

The following gave me special assistance in procuring photographs used in this volume: Franklin A. Barrett, Otto Benesch, Rudolf

Berliner, T. G. Burn, Alister Campbell, Ernest Stanley Dodge, E. Edwards, Webster Evans, J. P. van Goidsenhoven, Carl Hernmarck, Soame Jenyns, Jonkvrouwe Dottoressa C. H. de Jonge, Robert Kloster, Arthur Lane, Frank B. Lenz, Igo Levi, Giuseppe Liverani, H. Rissik Marshall, Richard B. K. McLanathan, Charles F. Montgomery, Stephen T. Riley, and Stig Roth.

I wish also to thank Mrs. Arthur A. Houghton, Jr., for letting me study at length and in detail her extraordinary collection of China-Trade teapots—a study which greatly facilitated my work in classifying the porcelain in Mrs. McCann's collection.

Marshall B. Davidson, Editor of Publications of the Metropolitan Museum, not only aided me in his official capacity, but through his wide knowledge of the China Trade with respect to the American market proved a most rewarding critic. James Thomas Flexner, another historian of American life and culture, also commented helpfully on my manuscript.

Agnes D. Peters, who edited my *Early Florentine Designers and Engravers*, was again the principal editor of the present volume. Too much credit cannot be given her. Especially is this so in connection with the general planning of the presentation of Part II, wherein the McCann collection is described in some detail. Marshall B. Davidson and Olga Krupen supervised the final stages of the book's production. To them, and to John E. Booth, who edited most of Part I, my thanks for their effective help. Olga Raggio and Gertrude Howe are among the many others to whom I am indebted. I should finally like to point out that the handsome design of the book is the work of Peter Oldenburg.

NOTE Sources of the quotations and the illustrations in the text are given in the Acknowledgments and References, page 225.

PART ONE

CHINA-TRADE PORCELAIN

CHINGTECHEN

Chingtechen has always been an extraordinary town. There still is no other at all like it. In Kiangsi, a quiet agricultural province of inner China, well protected, remote from the world, and distant from the main routes of travel, rises this center of belching furnaces. Clouds of smoke from their chimneys fill the sky, and at night their flames spew forth into the darkness. In an industrialized Western city such a sight might not be remarkable, but in China, especially inner China, such a sight is astounding, and has been so for centuries to the few Westerners who have visited there (Fig. 1).

Chingtechen is a dedicated place. All its life and energy have steadily gone into the making of a single product. As Lyons is the silk center, as Detroit is the motor city, so Chingtechen is the town of porcelain. It has been the town of porcelain for over two thousand years. Although its greatest achievements date from the fourteenth through the eighteenth centuries, its preeminence has continued virtually without interruption to modern times. Among its many porcelain products were the wares made specially for export to the West. And so it is here that our story of China-Trade porcelain begins.

Chingtechen can be reached from the coast of China by traveling up the Yangtze River to Kiukiang. From there one crosses Poyang Lake to the city of Jaochow, which is watered by the river Chang. Thirty miles up this stream is Chingtechen.

The first Western description of Chingtechen comes from Father d'Entrecolles, a Jesuit missionary, who came upon the place with an amazement born of seeing something new, unimagined, and completely unrelated to anything in his Occidental experience. The missionary's vivid picture of Chingtechen is set down in a letter he wrote in 1712:

The sight with which one is greeted on entering through one of the gorges consists of volumes of smoke and flame rising in different places, so as to define all the outlines of the town; approaching at nightfall, the scene reminds one of a burning city in flames . . .

This description of Chingtechen surely deserves an honored place in the annals of romantic literature. One of the very first of its kind, it also proved to be long remembered, as is shown by the following passage from Longfellow's poem *Kéramos*, written in the mid-nineteenth century:

And bird-like poise on balanced wing
Above the town of King-te-tching,
A burning town, or seeming so,—
Three thousand furnaces that glow

Incessantly, and fill the air
With smoke uprising, gyre on gyre,
And painted by the lurid glare
Of jets and flashes of red fire.

While celebrated in the verse and prose of other lands, paradoxically enough Chingtechen never has been fully honored or recognized in China. There are few references to it in Chinese poetry, although when they do occur they have been highly effective. Chu Yuan-tso, Director of the Imperial Factory at Chingtechen in the late fifteenth century, was the author of the following lines:

Ten thousand *li* from the Palace gates, I live behind a scarlet door. Mountain peaks are spread around and mists appear like flowers in spring. Day

FIGURE I *Chingtechen (or King-te-tching) and the surrounding region*

Detail from a map of Kiangsi province. From Du Halde, *Description . . . de la Chine . . .*, Paris, 1735

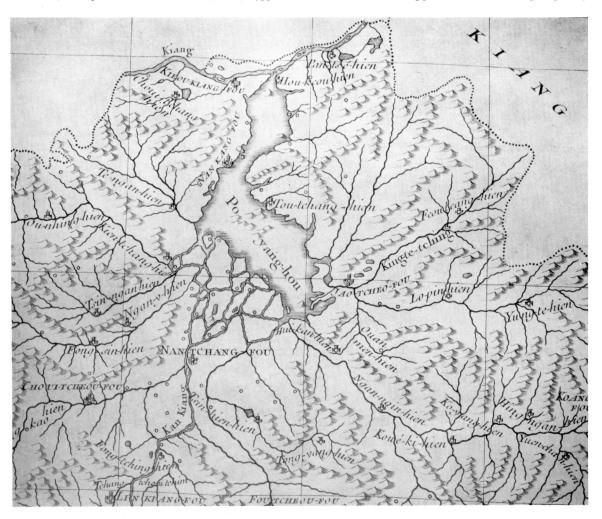

FIGURE 2   *View of Chingtechen, 1920*

and night the chimneys pour out smoke and fire. The sun rises from a purple sea and the kilns seem like a forest about me.

Despite its continuous industrial activity through the centuries, Chingtechen has never gained the status of a city. This, however, is hardly surprising in China. Since trade in general has always been disdained by the dominant mandarin class, Chingtechen's attainments as a manufacturing center inevitably passed unnoticed. The town, moreover, has lacked that essential dignifying element of Chinese cityhood, a surrounding wall. It has lacked, too, the presence of the literati, that is to say, that class of men of education and culture which gave to a locality a distinction the Chinese prize. Furthermore, Chingtechen depended politically and economically on Nanchang, the polished and sophisticated provincial capital.

Unlike Chingtechen, Nanchang "has always produced a great Number of Literati, and is full of Persons of Distinction," another Jesuit of the 1700s, Jean Baptiste du Halde, recorded. "The *Vice-Roy* keeps his Court in this City, where there are considerable Officers and Magistrates." Nanchang was also the home of a number of exiled Ming princes, and they lent a further distinction to the place. It was, moreover, the provincial trading center, and the sale of porcelain was its biggest business. The merchants of Chingtechen used the town as their chief market place, and dealers from all the provinces of China came there to buy porcelain.

Although not called a city by the Chinese, Chingtechen had over a million inhabitants in the eighteenth century, according to Father d'Entrecolles. Even allowing for the possibility that such an estimate was a bit high, Chingtechen was certainly one of the principal urban centers of China and actually one of the largest cities of the entire eighteenth-century world. In 1712, when D'Entrecolles reported on its size, it was apparently larger than London and Paris, both of which numbered little more than half a million people. In all Europe only Constantinople could claim as large a population. Comparisons are often dangerously misleading; they can also be revealing. Here they suggest the extraordinary size of this town, quite unknown beyond the borders of China, with its vast population, numbering twice that of contemporary

4

Paris, occupied in making porcelain wares for China and the entire civilized world.

Further passages from Father d'Entrecolles's letter describing the town are to be found in Du Halde's "General History of China" (the name commonly given to the English translation, made in 1738, of his *Description . . . de la Chine* of 1735). We give them as they appear in this early translation, for though they may be somewhat discursive they have all the flavor of direct observation. In this way we may attempt to visualize Chingtechen through the eighteenth-century eyes of Du Halde's "on-the-spot reporter," Father d'Entrecolles.

King-te-ching [Chingtechen] extends a League and a half along a fine River, and is not a Heap of Houses as might be imagin'd, but the Streets are very long, and intersect each other at certain Distances, without a Scrap of waste Ground to spare in it. The Houses themselves are rather too close [and, as is noted elsewhere in this description, "take up a great deal of Room and contain a prodigious Multitude of Workmen"]; and the Streets too narrow; in passing thro' them one would think himself in the middle of a Fair, and they ring with the Cries of Porters, who are clearing way.

It is considerably dearer living here than at *Zhau-chew* [Jaochow], because whatever is consum'd must be brought from other Places, even to the Wood for supplying the Furnaces with Fewel, which at present comes from near three hundred Miles Distance; but notwithstanding the Dearness of Provisions, it is the Refuge of an infinite Number of poor Families, who have no Means of subsisting in the neighboring Towns. They find Employment here for Youths and weakly Persons; there are none, even to the Lame and Blind, but what get their living here by grinding Colours. Anciently they rekon'd no more than three hundred Porcelain Furnaces at this Place, but at present they amount to about five hundred.

King-te-ching stands in a Plain, surrounded with high Mountains; that on the East-side, against which it is built, forms, without, a kind of Semi-circle. The Mountains on the Sides give Passage to two Rivers, one of them is small, the other very large [the Chang]; which unite and make an handsome Port, within a League of the Place, in a vast Basin, where it loses a good Deal of its Rapidity. One sees sometime two or three Rows of Barks, following one another the whole length of this Space . . .

Strangers are not suffer'd to be at *King-te-ching*: whoever has not Acquaintances in the Place to answer for his Behavior, must lodge at Night in his Barks. This Regulation, join'd to that which is observ'd at Day and Night in the Borough itself, the same as in the Cities, keeps all in good Order; and establishes perfect Security in a Place, whose Riches would otherwise make it liable to the Attempts of an infinite Number of Robbers.

Two centuries later another traveler set down his impressions of Chingtechen, and the similarity of the observations of the two men is striking in view of the span of time that separated them. In the *National Geographic Magazine* in 1920 Frank B. Lenz began an account of his visit to Chingtechen by noting the quiet pleasures of approaching the town by water, with the river banks "dotted with pine and camphor trees, while occasional groves of bamboo in lighter green add a charm and beauty difficult to describe." With him we seem to venture into the magic landscape of some ancient Chinese scroll painting.

On nearing the town Mr. Lenz discovered that the bed of the stream appeared to be paved with countless fragments of porcelain—mute, glittering records of the mistakes of many generations of potters. The smoke billowing from the kilns of Chingtechen impressed him, and he was amazed to find in this remote section of the world a scene so reminiscent of the smoky, industrialized cities of the West (Fig. 2).

He found the town still completely dedicated to porcelain making, although the decline in manufacturing in the past century and a half had reduced the population. He described Chingtechen as a busy, industrial city of 300,000 people. He reported that its small concessions to modernity were proving irksome to them. Rickshaws were then considered to be unpopular innovations which were creating intolerable traffic problems. But even then, as late as 1920, there was not a single newspaper, daily or weekly, published in Chingtechen. Clearly the literati had not yet moved in.

[2]

To look at a map is to discover one reason for Chingtechen's pre-eminence in manufacturing porcelain; to examine the earth and rocks and the quality of the waters nearby is to discover another.

Chingtechen is favorably located on the widespread network of inland waterways—rivers and canals—for which China is famous. As a result, the essential raw materials not immediately available could readily be brought to the factories, and the finished products could just as easily be dispatched to the farthest reaches of the Empire or started on their way to distant lands.

As to the quality of the water itself, it may be—although there is no proof for this—that the clear mountain water of the Chang River, when used in the refining of the porcelain clays, subtly helped to form the character of these basic earths. Father du Halde thought so. In his "General History" he observed that "it seems that the Water of the Place where the *China* is made, contributes to its Beauty and Goodness, for they do not make so good elsewhere, altho' they employ the same Materials." Mr. Lenz, too, commented on the nature of the water, contrasting the Chang's crystal clarity with the muddy yellowness of Lake Poyang and the Yangtze. Water was also used as power to operate the countless small mills that ground the granitic rocks into the smooth clay known as petuntse, and this power the Chang and its tributaries were able to furnish.

As for the earth and rocks, it was Chingtechen's good fortune to be uniquely located with respect to the materials needed for porcelain manufacture. There are two clays which together compose the body of Chingtechen ware.

One of these clays, petuntse, is man made. It is formed by crushing a granitic rock (felsite, or petrosilex) until, with the addition of water, the mass attains the consistency of clay. The other, a natural clay of a fine texture and a remarkably white cast, is called kaolin, or China clay. Geologically it is akin to petuntse, for it represents the partial decomposition of the same rock from which petuntse is derived. The basic difference between the two is that the quartz which forms a considerable part of the petuntse stone is not present in the kaolin. When joined together in a mixture, petuntse and kaolin reinforce each other remarkably. With its distinctive quartz content, the petuntse renders the mixture more readily fusible; kaolin makes it more susceptible to modeling. The glaze used to coat the vessels as they emerge from the potters' hands is made largely of petuntse, and because of its quartz content it fuses completely to form the hard glassy surface that is characteristic of porcelain. In the light of the origins of both petuntse and kaolin, the stony hardness of porcelain is understandable.

Both the petuntse rock and the kaolin have always been available in deposits not too far distant from Chingtechen. Originally, when porcelain was first being made at Chingtechen, petuntse was mined in the nearby countryside. In the eighteenth century, however, petuntse was found most richly in the mountains along the course of the Chang River. According to Father d'Entrecolles, a considerable number of small boats "come down from Ki-mên [a mining town some distance up the Chang] laden with *Pe-tun-tse* and *Kao-lin* made up into bricks." Incidentally, the word petuntse means "little clay bricks." The word kaolin is derived from the name Kao Ling, a mountainous district some miles to the northwest of Chingtechen which was once rich in the material.

Fuel in the form of firewood and straw also reached Chingtechen by river boat. Since it took ten tons of fuel to maintain a single kiln at the high temperature of 1500° centigrade for the twenty-four hours necessary for the manufacture of porcelain, countless river craft were required to keep all the kilns in town supplied. In the early days of porcelain manufacture, fuel was obtained from nearby forests. By the eighteenth century, however, these sources had been depleted. Consequently, some of the river craft brought their loads from sources hundreds of miles distant.

In a like manner Chingtechen's finished products were sent to market by the water route. Those destined for the northern regions of China, foremost among them the wares made for the Imperial court at Peking, were first shipped to Kiukiang, the nearby Yangtze port. They were then transported down the Yangtze to Chinkiang, and thence by the inland Grand Canal, all the way to Tientsin.

FIGURE 3 *Transporting porcelain from Chingtechen to Canton over the Meiling Pass*

Chinese painting. Probably late XVIII century. British Museum

Those destined for the south of China—and most of the wares intended for the China Trade were shipped to Canton, the greatest of the southern cities—were first dispatched to Nanchang, where they were transferred to craft operating on the Kan River. In this manner they were conveyed as far south as the town of Nananfu near the border of Kiangsi province. Then, for a short distance the way lay overland, through a mountain pass "so steep," we learn from the "General History," "that in some Places they have cut it in the form of stairs." This was the ancient Meiling Pass, which formed the gateway between Canton and the north (Fig. 3). The town of Namyung at the southern end of the Pass was on a tributary of the North River, which flowed past Canton. From Namyung on, the trip was a simple matter. Altogether

the distance from Chingtechen to Canton was about six hundred miles, the approximate distance from New York to Detroit.

Another route connected Chingtechen and Canton, one that lay entirely by water: down the Yangtze River to Nanking, near the river's mouth; thence by ocean-going junks to Canton. It was longer than the route of the Meiling Pass, and on the high seas piracy was ever a menace. Yet it seems to have been used, and it may be for this reason that the wares of Chingtechen with underglaze decorations were often known in the West as Nanking or Nankeen china, after the port where they were transshipped.

[3]

Although Chingtechen had but one product, it had a great many small factories. During the period of the China Trade about five hundred independent kilns were in operation, and there seem to have been from three to four thousand factories, for the ratio between kiln and factory was reckoned as being about one to eight. Father d'Entrecolles gave us a picture of how the factories looked: "In a Place encompass'd with Walls, they have built vast Pent-Houses [sheds], wherein appears abundance of Earthen Vessels, in rows one above another. Within this inclosure an infinite number of Workmen live and work, each having his particular Task." Photographs used to illustrate A. D. Brankston's *Early Ming Wares of Chingtechen* (see Figs. 4–6), showing how porcelains were made, would serve to document Father d'Entrecolles's description, despite the passage of two centuries.

Lacking power-driven equipment, the managers of the Chingtechen factories had developed the technique of dividing the work into many separate operations, each of which they assigned to a particular group of workers. Under this system, not unlike the assembly-line method of our own day, each man had to learn only one particular operation. Although he might be completely without skill in all the other phases of the work, he could carry out this one operation to perfection.

In his letter of 1712 Father d'Entrecolles gave

FIGURE 4 *"From loaves of clay to cups;" the making of porcelain in Chingtechen in 1937*

a succinct account of the several stages of porcelain manufacture. He noted that some pieces were made with the wheel and that others were made solely by the use of molds. He called those made on the wheel "smooth" ware (the Chinese used the term "round" ware, perhaps a better expression, since it described porcelains basically circular in shape). D'Entrecolles pictured the making of a typical piece of smooth ware, the teacup. The teacup was very imperfect when it came from the wheel, not unlike the crown of a hat before it is formed on the block (Fig. 4). The man at this, the first, wheel was concerned only

FIGURE 5 *Applying glaze to a bowl (Chingtechen, 1937)*

with giving the cup its height and width. Another workman added its foot—a daub of clay. Then it passed to a third, who placed it on an appropriately shaped mold attached to a wheel, which gave it its definitive form. In such a manner, from one refining process to another, it passed from hand to hand until it had been glazed and placed to dry, ready for firing (Figs. 5 and 6).

Father d'Entrecolles noted that "it is surprising to see with what Swiftness these Vessels run thro' so many Hands. Some affirm that a Piece of *China*, by the time it is bak'd, passes the Hands of seventy Workmen; which I can easily believe after what I have seen my self."

The role of the wheel is well known in the history of ceramics. The role played by the potter's mold in the completion of porcelains that had already been formed on the wheel may come as a surprise to any but a specialist in the subject. T'ang Ying, who was a contemporary of Father d'Entrecolles and Director of the Imperial Factory from 1736 to 1743, just at the moment when the production of export porcelain was approaching its height, described the mold's essential function when he wrote that in "the manufacture of round ware each several piece has to be repeated hundreds or thousands of times: without moulds it would be most difficult to make the pieces all exactly alike."

Regarding another, more complicated type of mold, the piece-mold, made for the manufacture of vessels, such as tureens and platters, which were not designed on a central axis, Father d'Entrecolles had this to say:

To hasten a Work that is bespoken, a great number of Moulds are made, for employing several Companies of Workmen at the same time. If care be taken of these Moulds, they will last a long while; and a merchant, who has them ready by him for those sorts of Works which *Europeans* require, can deliver his Goods much sooner and cheaper, and yet gain considerably more by them, than another who has them to make.

It may be noted that, just as with the die-cutters in modern industry, the mold-makers in China formed a distinct group; only a few of the Chingtechenese qualified for this exacting occupation.

Besides the use of these two types of molds, one other example of the production-line manufacture of porcelain is to be found in the manner in which painted decorations were applied to the clay surfaces. Although this system held only for certain of the China-Trade porcelains, such as the blue-and-white wares, it remains a striking example of the working methods followed in Chingtechen.

Father d'Entrecolles noted that "the Painting part is divided, in the same Work-house, among

FIGURE 6 *Porcelain bowls, after having been formed on the wheel and glazed, are stored on shelves to dry (Chingtechen, 1937).*

a great number of Operators. It is the sole Business of one to strike the first colour'd Circle, near the Edges of the Ware; another traces the Flowers, which are painted by a third; it belongs to one to draw Rivers and Mountains, to another Birds and other Animals: As for the Figures of Men, they are commonly the worst done of all." To lessen the sting of this last observation, the author felt impelled to add that certain landscapes and plans of towns which were brought from Europe to China were of such mediocre quality that Westerners could hardly mock at the Chinese for the manner in which they represented themselves in their paintings.

The novel system which was developed at Chingtechen for the making of porcelain had serious shortcomings. Chief among them was the fact that individual effort was necessarily subordinated to a program carefully planned to include the participation of a multitude of workers. Nothing could be done spontaneously, and many things were done mechanically. On the other hand, it made possible the faithful reproduction in porcelain of the same forms and patterns as many times as desired—countless times, if necessary. And it was precisely because of this that the great export trade could flourish in the eighteenth century.

[4]

Porcelain is said to have been produced in Chingtechen, or Ch'ang-nan, as it was then called, as early as the Han dynasty (206 B.C.–A.D. 220). It was not until the Sung dynasty (960–1280) that the town became Chingtechen, a name chosen to honor one of the early Sung monarchs, Ching-te (1004–1007).

With the Ming dynasty (1368–1644) Chingtechen entered its golden age of artistic achievement. By that time the Imperial Factory had been permanently established there, and wares were sent annually to the Emperor at Peking. The Imperial Factory seems, in fact, to have been the key to the town's subsequent brilliant history, for the exacting standards set for the Imperial works were passed on to the town's many private industries.

The time of the Ming emperor Hsüan-tê (1426–1435), when form and decoration were synthesized into one harmonious expression, marks a high point in the annals of porcelain manufacture. In the words of the early-seventeenth-century writer Shen Te-fu, "during the Hsüan-tê period potters were inspired by Heaven to produce works of subtle meaning and supreme artistry." Painted wares were then usually decorated under the glaze in cobalt blue, but as time went on, other hues, including a variety of post-glaze enamel colors, were employed.

In the seventeenth century, during the period of transition from the Ming dynasty to that of the Ch'ing (1644–1912), there was a brief interlude of trouble. The town of Chingtechen was leveled by fire in 1675, only to rise again from the ashes of its own kilns, thanks to the support of one of China's greatest men, the Ch'ing emperor K'ang-hsi (1662–1722). With his help the town turned its collective genius to the task of producing porcelains of unparalleled splendor and richness. A profusion of exciting new wares appeared; colors assumed a peacock brilliance, and shapes were as complicated as potters could invent. Above all, this age of K'ang-hsi has long been known for the ware called, because of the predominance of the color green in its boldly painted patterns, *famille verte*.

K'ang-hsi was followed by his son Yung Chêng, who ruled from 1723 to 1735, and by his grandson Ch'ien Lung, who ruled from 1736 to 1795. Accurately reflecting the spirit of K'ang-hsi's successors, the porcelain of the day suggested a life that was assured, relaxed, and rather dull. It showed, as we also know from history, that the Celestial Empire had reached the dangerous age of serene maturity. It was the age that had been symbolically ushered in by the all but incredible Festival of the Old Men, held in 1721 on the occasion of K'ang-hsi's sixtieth anniversary as ruler, when duly selected representatives of the aged of all China were gathered together in the Forbidden City to celebrate with their Emperor. This period may be said to have been symbolically closed by an equally bizarre repetition of the festival in 1785, a feast in honor of Ch'ien Lung's fifty years as emperor. Never before and never since have old men anywhere been so honored as on these two occasions.

Throughout this period the ceramics industry at Chingtechen flourished. Commercial success, however, was accompanied by a decline in esthetic interest. In keeping with the spirit of the times the highly spirited *famille verte* style gave way to the almost rococo elegancies of the ware known as *famille rose*, which in popularity then surpassed all other decorative styles in porcelain.

It was during the fabulous Age of the Old Men that most of the China-Trade porcelain was made, and much of this export ware was no more than a subspecies of *famille rose*.

Unlike the porcelains made for the Chinese domestic market, however, those made for export to the West received their final enamel decorations in Cantonese workshops. Thus, in order to understand the further developments in the story of China-Trade porcelain—the final steps in its manufacture, and the actual process of marketing and exporting the finished article—we now turn our attention from Chingtechen to the great port city of Canton.

THE OPENING
OF TRADE
WITH
THE WEST

Canton, described by Father du Halde in the eighteenth century as one of the most populous and opulent cities in China, was the hub of the old China Trade. To it flowed from all the provinces of the Empire the teas, the silks, the lacquers, and the myriad other riches of the land, prominent among which were porcelains. To Canton from the outside world came merchants seeking these riches. Only to Canton could they come, for, unique among Chinese port cities, which usually barred all foreigners, Canton admitted them, at least to her outskirts.

Not only was the export porcelain ordered, prepared for shipment, and finally loaded aboard Western vessels at Canton, but it was here too that most of the finer porcelains which had been dispatched from Chingtechen received their final enamel decorations. In many instances the designs had previously been selected by the purchasers in Europe.

This great trading center of southern China is located some eighty miles up the Pearl River. With respect to its situation on an inland waterway it is like the port of London on the Thames. In the eighteenth century it was a walled city, and was set back a short distance from the northerly bank of the river (Fig. 7).

The water front and the suburbs flanking the city were areas of commerce, and only here were foreigners admitted. Set in these suburbs along the riverbank was a connected series of buildings housing the various East India Companies and individual private traders (or factors) together with the Cantonese merchants who dealt with them. These buildings were called factories (or *hongs*), and they represented Europe's tiny but portentous beachhead on the shores of China.

The sight of this mercantile outpost left a vivid impression on all those who visited Canton in the days of the China Trade. One of these visitors, William Hickey, who was at Canton in 1769, noted his impressions of the port in his *Memoirs*:

. . . the view of the city as you approach it is strikingly grand, and at the same time picturesque.

12

The magnitude and novelty of the architecture must always surprise strangers. The scene upon the water is as busy a one as the Thames below London Bridge, with this difference, that instead of our square-rigged vessels of different dimensions you have junks . . . Nothing appears more extraordinary to the eyes of a stranger at Canton than the innumerable boats of different sizes with which the river is covered for many miles together.

About half a mile above the City . . . is a wharf, or embankment, regularly built of brick and mortar, extending more than half a mile in length, upon which wharf stands the different factories or

FIGURE 7   *The port of London and the harbor of Canton*

Scenes in the border of a China-Trade plate bearing the arms of Lee of Caton. Before 1734. English market. This plate is a recent purchase for the McCann collection, The Metropolitan Museum of Art

FIGURE 8 *The riverside Hongs at Canton*

ABOVE and RIGHT: Punch bowl decorated at Canton for the American market. Early XIX century. Lent to The Metropolitan Museum of Art by Mrs. H. Edward Dreier, Mrs. George B. B. Lamb, and Mrs. Thomas Louden

places of residence of the Supercargoes [of the East India Companies], each factory having the flag of its nation on a lofty ensign staff before it. At the time I was in China they stood in the following order, First, the Dutch, then, the French, the English, the Swedes, and last, the Danes.

Other details are recorded by another traveler to the East, Sir George Staunton, who was in Canton in 1793 with Lord Macartney's Embassy:

The handsome factories of the different nations of Europe trading to it, situated in a line along the river, outside the walls of the city, each with its national flag flying over it [Fig. 8], contrast with the Chinese buildings, and are an ornament to the whole. The numbers of the strangers to be seen in the suburbs, while their ships are unloading and loading in the river; their various languages, dresses, and characteristic deportment, would leave it almost a doubt, if a judgment were to be formed

from that part of the town, to what nation it was belonging.

The neighborhood of the foreign factories is filled with storehouses for the reception of European goods until they are disposed of to the natives, or Chinese goods for exportation until shipped. The front of almost every house is a shop; and the shops of one or more streets are laid out chiefly to supply the wants of strangers.

Major Samuel Shaw, who was at Canton during 1784–1785, and who was the first citizen of the United States to engage in the China Trade, observed in his *Journals* that "the limits of the Europeans are extremely confined; there being, besides the quay, only a few streets in the suburbs, occupied by the trading people, which they are allowed to frequent" (Fig. 9). Moreover, Shaw added, "Europeans, after a dozen years' residence, have not seen more than what the first month presented to view."

The great China Trade was conducted within this restricted area of considerably less than a quarter of a square mile. There, for more than a hundred years, beginning early in the eighteenth century, the various individual traders and East India Companies carried on their business under conditions unparalleled in modern commercial history. They were segregated in a tiny area

outside the city walls, they could deal only in that one city, and they were faced with various exasperating systems of controls, taxes, and tribute. They had scant opportunity to learn that there were precedents for all these practices in Canton's ancient past.

Despite these restrictions, which they found onerous and humiliating, the Europeans trading under the walls of Canton were able to engage in a vast and profitable business. In 1794, to cite one successful year, the exports from Canton to England alone were reckoned to have amounted to over £1,500,000. At the end of the eighteenth century the business transacted at Canton was considered to be the richest part of England's foreign trade. Meanwhile, various other European nations and, after the Revolutionary War, the United States were sharing in the trade carried on there, although to a lesser extent.

[2]

Canton's history as a trading center reaches far back into China's past. Long before the arrival of the first Portuguese adventurers, the merchants of Canton had been engaged in dealing with various Asiatic traders. Since this early trade was to have a bearing upon the development of the China Trade of the eighteenth cen-

tury, it forms an integral part of our narrative.

T'ien-Tsê Chang, in his *Sino-Portuguese Trade from 1514 to 1644*, has pointed out that the seaport of Canton, because of its favored geographical position, was the first Chinese city to be visited by foreign ships and that between 250 and 300 A.D. travelers had already arrived there from western Asia. These early adventurers, who may have been Persians or Arabs, introduced the cultivation of jasmine on Cantonese soil. Although theirs is the first recorded instance of the presence of foreign traders in

FIGURE 9 *New China Street at Canton*

Lithograph by L. P. A. Bichebois after a drawing by Lauvergne. About 1835

15

Canton, others from the East Indies and Malaya may well have been there at a still earlier date. Other seaports on the China coast also shared in the early trade with foreigners, but Canton's role seems on the whole to have been the most continuous and the most important. Canton's chief rival during these early days was Ch'üanchow, a port not far from Amoy and known to Marco Polo as Zayton.

During the centuries that followed the arrival of the first merchants from abroad, foreign trade seems to have become increasingly important in the life of the city, which in due course developed into one of the leading centers of the realm. Japan, Southeast Asia, the Indies, and even India and Arabia were counted among her customers. Canton was truly an international market.

To facilitate this growing commerce it became necessary to allow foreigners to remain at least temporarily on Chinese soil, even if such a concession ran counter to the custom of the land. Hence, long before the arrival of the first European merchants, foreigners were permitted to live in a settlement of their own, set apart from the Chinese themselves but adjacent to the trading center. Foreign colonies seem to have been established in Canton as early as the middle of the seventh century. By the year 758 the Muhammadan colony there was so powerful that its members, in conflict with the Chinese, were able to burn the city and make off with its wealth. Later on other Moslems again settled there, and we learn from Ibn Battúta, an Arab visitor of the second half of the fourteenth century, that these had their cathedral mosque, hospice, and bazaar, as well as their own judge and sheik. At this early period, therefore, we can see the development of a long-lasting Chinese policy with regard to strangers which was to find its final expression during the eighteenth century in the famous row of factories ranged along the Pearl River.

The Imperial government was directly responsible for this and every other policy designed to promote and control the early foreign trade. For it recognized that trade abroad not only furthered industry at home but that it helped to fill the Imperial coffers through duties, tribute, and taxes.

During the T'ang dynasty (618–906) a tax agency known as the Bureau of the Trading Junks had been installed at Canton. Through it the Imperial government was able both to control and to tax the traders. This agency continued to function through the Sung dynasty (960–1280). Its procedures may be compared to those followed in the eighteenth century with respect to Western shipping.

Another income-producing device was tribute. Since the Emperor existed as a godlike element within the body politic, far above all the pettinesses of daily life, it was not thought seemly that he should be associated—even indirectly—with such mundane matters as the taxation of "barbarians." So it came about as time went on that the Imperial government came to prefer tribute—which signified vassalage—to direct imposts. Following the example of representatives of foreign states and with Imperial approval traders began to present themselves as tribute bearers, their tribute usually taking the form of gifts of the specialties and curiosities of their own countries.

The procedure seems to have become fairly general. In 1308 the Ministers of the Grand Council of China stated that "within the last half year, over 1200 messengers [bearing tribute] have traveled over the Kiangsu, Chekiang, and Hangchow post-roads." Since tribute was then transported at the expense of the state, unexpected costs were sometimes incurred. The report of the Ministers went on ruefully to note that "a man [named] Sang-wu-pao-ho-ting . . . with some others brought as tribute lions, leopards, and hawks. To provide for the men and animals during the twenty-seven days [of their journey] had required more than 1300 catties [1,733 pounds] of meat!"

The variety of goods to be obtained in Canton's international market is indicated by a list of some of the principal items of export and import during the Sung dynasty (960–1280). There were "gold, silver, Chinese cash, lead, tin, piece-goods of silk of all colours, porcelain, cloth, scented wood and drugs, rhinoceros horns, ivory, coral, amber, strings of beads, 'pin' iron [the identity of this item is unknown; some say it may have been Indian steel], tortoise shell, cornelians, chü-ch'ü shells [from a species of enormous oyster], rock crystals, foreign cloth, ebony, sapan wood etc." Here, indeed, we have a summary inventory of the wealth of the Orient, tales of which were to penetrate to distant Europe and to rouse Western adventurers to seek a share of it.

[3]

The first of the Europeans to come to China in any numbers were the Portuguese, and they were followed by the Dutch and the English.

We have accounts of the early Portuguese voyages to the Orient from two Italians who joined Portuguese expeditions. In 1515, following a historic Portuguese voyage of discovery in 1514 to the island of Tunmen on the Cantonese coast, Giovanni da Empoli, an Italian who was then stationed at Cochin, India, in the service of Portugal, wrote that his comrades had "also discovered China, where men of ours have been who are staying here: which is [sic] the greatest wealth that there can be in the world . . . the great things are so many that come from there, that they are amazing; so that if I do not die, I hope before I leave here to take a leap thither to see the Grand Khan, who is the king, who is called the king of Cathay." In the same year another Italian, Andrea Corsali, wrote of the Chinese to Duke Giuliano de' Medici in Florence: "they are a people of great skill, and on a par with ourselves . . . During this last year some of our Portuguese made a voyage to China. They were not permitted to land; for they say 'tis against their custom to let foreigners enter their dwellings. But they sold their goods at a great gain . . ."

Giovanni da Empoli, who hoped "to take a leap thither to see the Grand Khan," spoke more like a modern adventurer than one of the Asiatic traders who had approached China circumspectly and had regarded the Emperor with reverential awe. What impressed this renaissance Italian, already stirred by the sensational successes of the Portuguese in India and the Indies, was the report of China's limitless wealth. In this lighthearted and highhanded approach of the soldier of fortune there was stored up a great deal of subsequent trouble for both Europeans and Chinese.

On their second Chinese voyage, made in 1517, the Portuguese proceeded up the Pearl River as far as the city of Canton. This time Giovanni da Empoli was indeed among the crew. Needless to say, however, his leap did not bring him to the Emperor. Actually, he caught fever while still in Canton and died there.

The arrival of this ship marked Canton's first experience with Europeans, and a fateful one it was, for immediately an untoward event occurred. Soon after the Portuguese vessel had dropped anchor without permission, in sight of the city walls, a terrifying salvo was fired from her cannons. Although the Portuguese endeavored to explain this salute to the Chinese as a sign of respectful greeting, the latter interpreted it in another way. Nevertheless, under the discreet leadership of the Portuguese captain Fernão Peres de Andrade, things thereafter seemed to go smoothly, and the ship departed laden with Chinese goods.

FIGURE 10 *View of the harbor at Macao*

Chinese painting. About 1840. Peabody Museum, Salem

As a group, however, the Portuguese were not trusted. Aside from the dubious impression they had made in Canton, rumors of their brutality in the Spice Islands reached China. Chinese opinion seemed to be confirmed by the actions of another Portuguese captain, Fernão's brother, Simão Peres de Andrade, who came to Canton in 1519 and whose ruthless, piratical acts left the

FIGURE 11   *The Portuguese in Japan*

ABOVE: A Portuguese carrack. BELOW: A Portuguese captain-major and his men. Scenes from a Japanese screen of the early XVII century. Collection of His Majesty the Emperor of Japan

peace-loving Chinese utterly outraged. By then the evil repute of the Europeans was general. China therefore decided to end her new troubles once and for all: Imperial orders summarily closed the port of Canton to all foreign shipping. It was not to be officially reopened until 1699.

The Cantonese nevertheless continued to desire foreign trade as ardently as did the Portuguese. After a lapse of several decades, during which trade was carried on surreptitiously and spasmodically from a number of coastal towns, the Portuguese managed in 1557 to form a settlement at Macao; and there they were allowed to remain (Fig. 10). From Macao Portuguese merchants were allowed to visit Canton to trade at the half-yearly sales taking place in January and June. Portugal has never since left this tiny, rocky promontory where, some eighty miles below Canton, the Pearl River flows into the China Sea. Since 1847 Macao has been a part of the Portuguese Empire.

While the Portuguese were being allowed to settle at Macao, the Chinese government, in order to discourage piracy among its own people, enacted a law making it a capital offense for any subject of the Empire to venture beyond the coastal waters. Because of this, all foreign shipping was left in Portuguese hands, and Portugal made the most of its golden opportunity: for the rest of the century all goods leaving Canton, whatever their destination, were carried in Portuguese bottoms. The Macao–Japan voyage, undertaken annually, was one of the richest sources of revenue for these Western traders (Fig. 11).

During this period of Portuguese ascendancy, the main axis of the East–West trade—the so-called grand trade—was Canton–Lisbon. It was by this route, which led around the Cape of Good Hope, that a considerable number of Chinese products reached the West. At Lisbon these commodities were distributed by merchants who had come there from the various countries of Europe.

Only a few of the porcelains that reached Europe in this manner have survived. Earliest among them is a two-handled cup of blue-and-

FIGURE 12

Chinese porcelain bottle, a forerunner of China-Trade wares. Made to Portuguese order and dated 1557. Victoria and Albert Museum, London

white porcelain of the Chia Ching period (1522–1566), bearing the date 1541 and an inscription in Portuguese. The cup, now in the collection of Baixo Alentejo, was made for Pero de Faria, who was the Portuguese governor of Malacca from 1537 to 1543. Only slightly later is the vessel from the same period in the Victoria and Albert Museum with the date 1557 in underglaze blue (Fig. 12).

There is also an extraordinary group of five pieces of blue-and-white porcelain of the Wan Li period (1573–1619) in the Metropolitan Museum of Art (see Fig. 13). These five porcelains are completely Chinese in form and decoration, and one of them bears the mark of the Emperor

Wan Li's reign. They eventually found their way to England, where, about 1585, they were set in elaborate silver-gilt mounts, an indication of how highly they were valued. It is believed that the pieces belonged to Queen Elizabeth's Treasurer, Lord Burghley.

The days of Portugal's Oriental splendor ended in the first half of the seventeenth century. The price of her conquests in India, the Indies, and China had been heavy, and small kingdom that she was, she could not in the long run pay either in men or in money the costs of upkeep for her far-flung possessions. Consequently, the seventeenth century was for her an era of frustration and of colonial decay.

As early as 1600 Portugal's supremacy in Far Eastern waters was challenged. In that year a Dutch fleet suddenly appeared in the area and proceeded to waylay and seize Portuguese galleons laden with costly Chinese goods. The cargo of one such ship, the *Catherina*, captured in 1602 in the Strait of Malacca, when brought to Amsterdam, created a sensation among the Dutch and sold for 3,400,000 guilders. Later, the oncoming Hollanders wrested the strategically important port of Malacca from the Portuguese, who until then had controlled the sea lanes from that stronghold. Thereafter the Portuguese at Macao found themselves far from a friendly base.

Moreover, the seventeenth century was an

FIGURE 13

Chinese porcelain bowl of the Wan Li period (1573–1619), with silver-gilt mounts added in England about 1585. The Metropolitan Museum of Art

age of turmoil within China itself, for one dynasty, that of the Ming emperors, was slowly perishing, and order was gradually restored to the realm only after the succession of the Ch'ing dynasty in 1644. During this period of change Canton was laid waste by warring factions, and for several decades trade languished. Yet somehow the Portuguese managed to fend off Dutch attacks and to maintain their precarious foothold at Macao, succeeding by means of judicious gifts and bribes in remaining on friendly terms with the Chinese. In spite of the increasing success of the Dutch, they were never entirely at a loss for Chinese trade.

[4]

The Dutch were actually led into the China Trade by European political events which took place during the latter part of the sixteenth century. In 1594 Spain was at war with Holland, and Philip II, who had become in 1580 the ruler of Portugal as well as Spain, closed the port of Lisbon to Dutch shipping. Henceforth, if the Dutch wished to obtain goods from the East Indies and from China at reasonable prices they had to look elsewhere. Since they had been the chief carriers of such merchandise from Lisbon to northern Europe, they determinedly sought a way to regain their lost trade.

Their plan was not long in evolving. Holland decided on no less venturesome a course than that of wresting the Oriental trade from both the Portuguese and the Spaniards, who, voyaging by way of Mexico and the Pacific, had been established in Manila since 1571. As an instrument for making their plan effective, the Hollanders in 1602 formed the Dutch East India Company, with a privately subscribed capital of 6,600,000 guilders. The Company gave its captains almost unlimited powers for dealing with any situation and authorized them to establish colonies. Their vessels were equipped to fight or trade as the occasion demanded (Fig. 14).

In the Far East the Dutch mapped out two chief areas of operation. One was the region of the East Indies. The other extended along the northern perimeter of the South China Sea and included the coast of China. In the first area the Hollanders were singularly successful. From their strategic positions astride the straits of Sunda and Malacca they were in control of the sea lanes to China, able not only to threaten every Portuguese craft sailing homeward from Macao but actually to curtail sharply the volume of the "grand trade" to Lisbon.

If in the China coast area the Hollanders were not so successful, their efforts were not entirely unrewarded. True, they were not able to engage directly in trade at Canton. They were turned back by Portuguese arms and intrigue when they approached Macao in 1604 and 1607, and again in 1622. In 1624, however, a Dutch fleet landed on the island of Formosa, establishing a settlement there which was profitably maintained until 1661. In 1638 they put over an even greater coup when they won the sole right to trade in Japan. On this later occasion they were able to oust the Macao-based Portuguese from that rich market.

The significance of these varied operations for our story is that from Formosa and Japan, as well as from various coastal and island ports, the Dutch were able to obtain large quantities of Chinese and other Oriental goods. Some of these were used in their local trade, which was known as "Indies to Indies"; others were shipped as part of the "grand trade" to the home port of Amsterdam, which in the seventeenth century was what Lisbon had been in the sixteenth and what London was destined to become in the eighteenth. Altogether it was a most flourishing era for the Dutch. In 1669, for instance, the year of the death of Rembrandt, the Dutch East India Company owned 150 trading ships and 40 warships and had a standing army of 10,000 men. The profits for that year were such that the stockholders received a dividend of no less than forty per cent.

In the global struggle for trade in the seventeenth century such high profits naturally did not accrue to men short in courage and stamina. A revealing contemporary impression of the men of the Dutch East India Company is found in

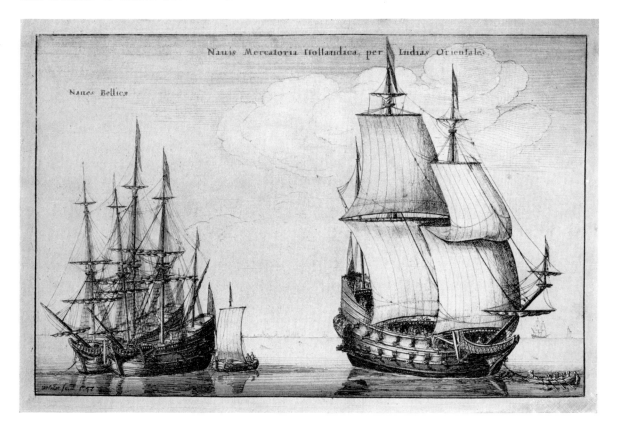

FIGURE 14   *Armed trading vessels of the Dutch East India Company*

Engraving by W. Hollar. Dutch, 1647. The Metropolitan Museum of Art

the *T'ai-wan Fu-chih*, a book compiled in the eighteenth century from earlier sources.

The people which we call Red-hair or Red barbarians are the Dutchmen. They are also called Po-ssu-hu. They live in the extreme west of the Ocean extending from Formosa . . . They are covetous and cunning and have good knowledge of valuable commodities and are clever in seeking profits. They spare not even their lives in looking for gain and go to the most distant regions to trade . . . If one meets them in the high seas, one is often robbed by them . . . Wherever they go, they covet rare commodities, and contrive by all means to take possession of the land.

Among the Chinese commodities sold at Amsterdam, none was more in demand than porce-

lain. In particular, the blue-and-white wares of the contemporary Ming and early Ch'ing dynasties were so much admired that the Dutch modeled their own Delft pottery after them. Much of the porcelain that came to Europe in the seventeenth century entered by way of Amsterdam, a trading center frequented by merchants from the various European capitals. So it was that even while the Dutch traders were excluded from Canton, they were influential in the porcelain trade.

[5]

As early as the Dutch, the English had their eyes fixed on the rich Far Eastern market. They had before them the challenging example of the Portuguese adventurers in that remote area. Indeed, their own ships had been engaged in trade at Lisbon for the commodities brought to Europe by the Portuguese. Philip II's closing of the port of Lisbon to the shipping of countries unfriendly to Spain in 1594, six years after the destruction of the Armada, had therefore inflicted a hardship on the English. So, like the Dutch, they determined to go to the source of supplies, to the Indies themselves, and there secure the spices and other goods so keenly wanted. Unwittingly, Philip had initiated a turn of events that was to have dire results for the future of his Portuguese and Spanish subjects trading in the Far East.

In 1599 a group of London capitalists asked permission of their government to found a company for trading in the Orient. Their declared aim was, "for the honour of our native cuntrey and for th' advauncement of trade of merchaundize within this realme of England, [to] set forthe a vyage this present year to the Est Indies and other ilandes and cuntries therabouts." The charter, however, was not granted until December 31, 1600. It was signed by Queen Elizabeth. The actual name of the company was "The Governor and Company of Merchants of London Trading into the East Indies."

The ships of the East India Company were soon in Far Eastern waters, trading successfully enough but in a minor way in the East Indies. Although for many years they did not venture to the more distant and inaccessible Canton, Canton was never forgotten. In 1627 a memorandum from Batavia, the Company's principal post in the Far East, to the home office in London stated the problem of commercial relations with the Chinese in its simplest terms:

Concerning the Trade of China, three things are especially made known unto the World.

The One is, the abundant trade it affordeth.

The Second is, that they admit no Stranger into their country.

The Third is, that Trade is as Life unto the Vulgar, which in remote parts they will seek and accommodate, with Hazard of all they have.

The first independent attempt of the English to trade at Canton came in 1637, when Captain Weddell arrived there with a fleet of four vessels. Weddell had been sent out not by the Company but by a rival English organization known as the Courteen Association, a short-lived joint-stock venture in which King Charles I had an interest. Upon his arrival, Weddell was forced to cool his heels just outside Canton for some months while the Portuguese, jealous of their prerogatives at Macao, encouraged the Cantonese to put the English off on various pretexts. The situation, which was understandably frustrating for the English, became serious when Weddell, "hazarding all he had," used his cannon against a Chinese fort.

This was a serious breach. It was up to the prospective trader to China to announce himself in a fashion more measured and consistent with the custom and law of the land. Living in the shadow of the haughty Chinese empire, the earlier Asiatic traders had understood this intuitively. The more impetuous Europeans were slow in grasping this basic principle. We have already seen that the Portuguese had made the same error of speaking with their armament. The Portuguese had eventually come to terms with the Chinese. Not until the eighteenth century, when the port of Canton was finally opened to Western traders, would the English and the Dutch be able to do the same.

During the remainder of the seventeenth century the English made various efforts to carry on trade from the ports of Amoy and Chusan in China and from Tongking in Indo-China and the island of Formosa. They had little success, for in these ports they were plagued by Oriental bureaucrats and unscrupulous merchants, while at sea they were menaced by their powerful and truculent Dutch rivals.

Despite all difficulties and disappointments, the English were not discouraged. Their persistence was finally rewarded when the government of K'ang-hsi, the first great ruler of the new Ch'ing dynasty, decided that it would be advantageous for his country to trade at Canton with other Europeans than the Portuguese. When the British ship *Macclesfield* arrived at Canton in 1699, she was able to take on a "full and rich cargo," including a small shipment of porcelains. A new era was about to begin.

THE EAST INDIA COMPANIES AND THE CHINA TRADE

The China Trade became a significant aspect of the world's commerce in the eighteenth century. Early in that period trade between East and West was put on an orderly basis and thereafter developed swiftly. The English, French, Dutch, Swedes, Danes, and others, including those late arrivals, the Americans, represented the West on the Canton market (Fig. 15).

Although these Western merchants were led to China in quest of porcelain, silks, and a variety of rare and precious commodities, they eventually found their chief reward in a staple of that country—tea. Virtually unknown to the West during the Age of Discovery, tea had risen to a commanding position as a commodity by the eighteenth century. Through the commerce in tea the China Trade in Canton attained vast dimensions, a stable market was created, and a regular shipping service came into being. All these developments were naturally favorable to the fullest possible expansion of the trade in chinaware, an enterprise that must be viewed within the framework of the whole tea-colored China Trade.

The early European traders had discovered that the use of tea was universal in China. Tea was used in solemn religious and political ceremonies; it also held an important position in the nation's daily life, and good cause there was for that. In a nation where drinking water had always to be boiled as a health measure, the simple addition of the tea leaf converted what for rich and poor alike had been a necessary nuisance into a pleasure.

In England in the China-Trade period a similar situation existed in respect to the water supply. The English had turned to beer, to which almost everyone was accustomed, even the children, who had their "small beer." It is not surprising, then, that when tea was brought to that country its simple preparation and agreeable flavor won it ready acceptance. Tea was China's inestimable gift to the English way of life.

The earliest shipments of tea to Europe were modest. In 1664 thirty-four ounces of it were purchased as a gift for Charles II by the Directors of the English East India Company—

perhaps from Dutch traders—at a cost of five pounds four shillings. Less than forty years later, however, the *Macclesfield* sailed from Canton with a cargo containing 20,000 pounds of tea. Year by year the demand grew. In 1723 five Company ships returned from Canton with over 900,000 pounds. In 1750 seven East India Company ships carried over 2,000,000 pounds of tea to England. And in the four years from 1769 to 1772 the average annual shipment rose to more than 10,000,000 pounds. By 1830, one of the last years of activity of the English East India Company in Canton, the tea export to England amounted to nearly 38,000,000 pounds. The average Canton price of good quality tea was then about a shilling a pound.

[2]

It was largely through this commerce in tea that the English came to control the lion's share of the China Trade throughout the eighteenth century.

The English were the first to establish a per-

FIGURE 15 *European merchants trading at Canton*

Ornamental detail from a map of the Province of Quang-Tong [Canton]. From Du Halde, *Description . . . de la Chine . . .* , Paris, 1735

manent factory at Canton—the year was 1715—and they made the most of it. In 1730, for example, there were 5 English ships, 2 French, and 1 Dutch at Canton. By 1790 there were 46 English ships, 2 French, 3 Dutch, 1 Danish, and 6 American. In 1810 there were, besides the few craft of other nations, 34 English ships and 37 ships from America. Although the English ships of that year were actually fewer than the American, they were about twice the size of the American ships and still carried the bulk of the trade.

En route to Canton the English ships (Fig. 16), and those of the other countries as well, followed the course that had been made known to the West by the great Portuguese sea captains of the Age of Discovery. The way lay down the Atlantic along the coast of Africa and around the southern tip of that continent into the vast reaches of the Indian Ocean. Some Company ships headed directly for the straits of Malacca or Sunda, through which they gained entry into the China Sea. Others first stopped for trade in various Indian ports. Ships pursuing the direct, nonstop course to Canton usually left England several months later than those routed by way of India.

From the time they arrived at Macao the traders were completely in the hands of Chinese officialdom. There each ship was boarded by a licensed Chinese pilot, who guided it to the Bogue, a station at the mouth of the Pearl River, where agents of the Imperial Commissioner of Customs (the powerful official known as the Hoppo) exacted certain port charges. These charges were of two sorts—measurage and a forced present—both of them indicative of the Chinese way of doing things.

Measurage was computed by multiplying a ship's length by its breadth. Length was considered to be the distance between the middle of the foremast and the middle of the mizzenmast; breadth, the distance from side to side close abaft the mainmast. The resulting figure was divided by ten and multiplied by a unit rate in Chinese currency. The average measurage charge was about 400 English pounds.

The forced present was a standard charge of

FIGURE 16   *The English East India Company merchant ship Haeslingfield [Hastingfield]*

ABOVE: The ship "in prosperity" (September 11, 1743). BELOW: The ship "in distress" (September 12, 1743). Decorations on a punch bowl painted in Canton for Robert Stockdall on January 1, 1744. The Metropolitan Museum of Art

about 650 English pounds. Such a "present" conformed to the ancient Chinese tradition of tribute giving. In earlier times of trade tribute had been rendered in the form of choice commodities. If in the eighteenth century it was bestowed in the form of silver, tribute it still remained—and a continuing source of irritation to the Europeans, who ever resented being required to pay it. The greater portion of it was theoretically for the Emperor; the rest of it was divided among a miscellany of petty officials, in-

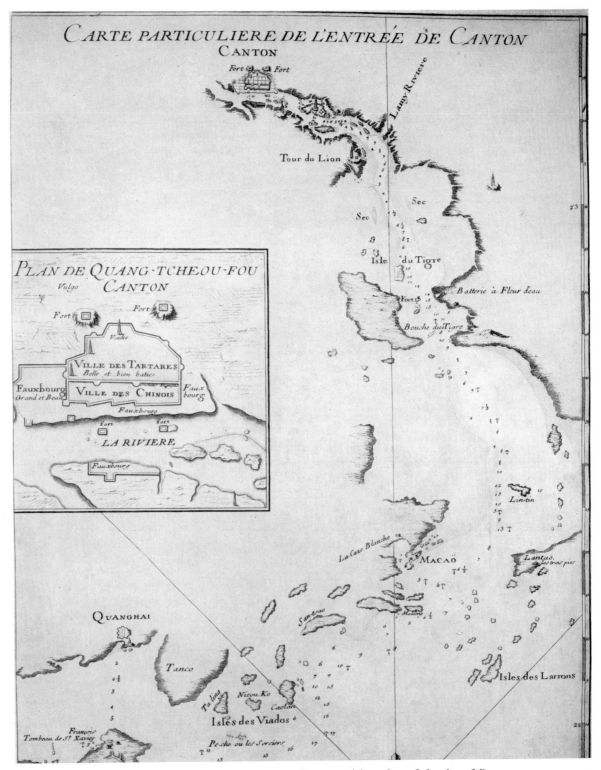

FIGURE 17   *The waterways leading to Macao and Canton, with a plan of the city of Canton*

The large island distinguished by a pagoda, shown northwest of Tour du Lion, is Whampoa. The Bogue is marked
"Bouche du Tigre." Map reproduced from Du Halde, *Description . . . de la Chine . . .* , Paris, 1735

26

cluding two "Tidewaiters," who were stationed aboard foreign vessels to act as informants for the Chinese as long as the traders remained at Canton.

From the Bogue the ships moved to Whampoa (Fig. 17), twelve miles below the city limits of Canton, where they finally dropped anchor. Once all charges were paid and final clearance received in the form of a "Chop," the ships' supercargoes were allowed to proceed in small craft to the Company's factory.

Whatever course the East Indiamen took, it was vital they all should reach Canton before the late fall had set in, if they were to profit from the favorable winds of the China Sea area. They had also to complete their trade in Canton by the end of the year, or at the very latest by the last of January, in order to take advantage of the winds of the winter season. For the monsoons of the late summer and fall blew steadily northwards, whereas those of the winter blew in the opposite direction. There are records of many Company ships, delayed for some reason or another, being unable "to save the monsoon" (that is, to take advantage of it). Vessels caught in this predicament were obliged to remain idle until the following season, thus losing a full year.

Foreign trade at Canton, therefore, was limited by the inflexible course of the monsoons to a period extending from midsummer until midwinter. During this trading season the foreign factories were beehives of activity. When the season was over, the factory area was as moribund as any fashionable summer resort in wintertime. The ships had departed; the flags along the water front were hauled down; the factories themselves were shut up. Even Europeans who, after the middle of the century, were permanently assigned to Canton were forced by Chinese authorities to leave. They passed the off-season in the comparative freedom of Macao, where Westerners were allowed to remain the year round.

[3]

A large measure of the success of the English Company is doubtless due to that unique group of men known as "supercargoes." Although the Company was an association of many investors, with its principal officers resident in London, the supercargoes were the key figures in it.

These men were not only the Company managers aboard ship and in port; to all intents and purposes they were the Company, high authority having been thrust upon them by force of circumstances. Because of the span of half the world separating the home office from Canton, because of the length of time generally consumed in a single round trip—about two years—and because the success of each Company venture lay entirely in the supercargoes' hands, it followed inevitably that they be granted the fullest possible scope for action.

They were no common breed of men. Their talents of necessity were varied and unusual. Each one had to be merchant, banker, linguist, and diplomat. In the early days of the trade, for example, the supercargoes had to have a knowledge of Portuguese if they would transact business at Canton. This situation changed after the establishment of the English factory there in 1715. The English soon became the most influential of the foreigners, and a strange new manner of speaking, "pidgin English" (business English), came into use, thus easing one aspect of the supercargoes' work. Even so, the Chinese government did its best to see that its language remained a mystery to the visitors from the West.

Company ships en route to Canton carried a considerable portion of their outbound capital in the form of silver coinage. Gold from China figured prominently in the return cargo. There was profit in gold, its cost in China being but two thirds of the mint price in Europe. Among his other skills, therefore, the supercargo had to possess a banker's knowledge of foreign exchange, and in transactions with the Chinese this was curiously intricate. If, for example, he were buying a bar of gold (known as a "shoe" on the Canton exchange) weighing 9.85 taels (the tael was $1\frac{1}{3}$ ounces) and of 97 touch in tested quality or fineness, to be sold at 4 above touch and paid for in ducatoons (silver coins of 96 touch minted in Venice), the reckoning, according to Hosea Ballou Morse, would be as follows:

9·85 taels of 97 touch is 10·274 taels 93 touch;
at 4 above touch is 101 taels silver for 10 taels gold,
or 99·485 taels current silver of 94 for this shoe of
    gold;
paid for in duccatoons of 96 touch,
    is 97·412 taels weight of duccatoons.

The supercargo had also to be a trained merchant, able to judge the value of tea and raw silks, and what quantities of these and other commodities on the market could be best acquired to produce the greatest profit at home. In his relations with the "Principalities and Powers of mundane rank," from Viceroy to shopman, the supercargo needed furthermore the diplomatic ability to cope with any number of bizarre situations, for the ways of the Chinese could be as unexpected as they were devious. As Morse has observed, the supercargo had to possess "not simply the courage to resist extortionate demands, but the skill to conduct a trade notwithstanding that such demands were made . . . All these qualities made it necessary that the supercargoes should be men of ability, of good education, and of incorruptible honesty."

The Company saw to it that their supercargoes were amply rewarded. In addition to their pay, which was the normal stipend of the English public servant, they were given an "Allowance" (profits from a portion of the stock on the ships), a "Permission" (the right to export on their own certain amounts in silver, and to return home with their investment in gold), and a "Privilege" (entitling them to carry on a private trade both on the outward and the homeward trip). This last, the Privilege, as we shall see in the next chapter, was to be of considerable importance in the development of the trade in porcelain.

These four sources of income—salary, Allowance, Permission, and Privilege—could be highly remunerative. It is estimated, for example, that G. M. Pitt, Chief Supercargo on the *Macclesfield*, in 1724 earned £5,890 sterling for his round-trip voyage to Canton. Such returns lured

a number of the most energetic men of the day into that venturesome career.

[4]

French ships had arrived at Canton at the very end of the seventeenth century, but the initial step towards the formation of regular trade was not taken until 1719, when the *Compagnie des Indes* was formed, replacing an older company that had been established early in the reign of Louis XIV. Following the example of their English rivals, the French set up a factory at Canton in 1728; unlike the English, they appointed a resident official at its head. Thereafter two or three ships traded annually in Canton.

There was, however, little stability in French foreign policy with respect to the Far Eastern trade. In 1769, for example, the government revised its point of view towards the whole venture by terminating the monopoly of the *Compagnie des Indes*, with the result that the French trade passed into the hands of independent merchants. On various occasions, also, French commerce with China was interrupted by war and revolution. As a result of the naval dominance of the British the Seven Years' War (1756–1763) and the Revolution and the Napoleonic Wars (1789–1815) were periods of no trade at all. On the whole, the French participation in the Canton market was ill-starred and sporadic.

Despite the brilliant record of the Dutch in Far Eastern waters during the seventeenth century, it was not until 1729 that their first ships, two Dutch East India Company vessels, reached Canton, where the English Company did its best to impede their activity. From then on the Hollanders engaged in a limited but effective trade. They established their factory in Canton in 1762, and throughout the second half of the century four or five of their ships visited there annually.

The first record of a Danish ship to arrive in Canton was in 1731. Thereafter two or three ships a year came faithfully to the Canton market. The Swedish East India Company sent its first ship there one year later, in 1732, and its trade during the remainder of the century was about the volume of that of the Danes.

The Imperial flag of Austria, somewhat like that of Panama in our own day, was the convenient cloak for ships and crews of divers nationalities seeking to avoid the stigma of an unpopular allegiance or the restrictions of national monopolies. Ostend was home port for the Imperialists, and as a result they were commonly known as "Ostenders." Though it was a nuisance to the old line Companies, the Ostend trade was never very large. Much of what the Ostenders exported—principally tea—was directed to the English market in clandestine competition with the monopoly of the English Company, for smuggling was a well-established occupation and, because of high English duties, a successful one.

An occasional Spanish ship also appeared at Canton, destined for Manila. From there Chinese goods were transshipped across the Pacific to the Mexican port of Acapulco, freighted across Mexico, and shipped, this time from Vera Cruz, to the Spanish home ports. From their base at Macao the Portuguese continued to maintain a lethargic trade that was of little consequence in the commercial annals of the times. Portuguese commerce remained a monopoly of the crown.

[5]

Until the outbreak of the Revolution the Americans had been obliged by British trade laws to secure all Oriental commodities by way of England. In so doing they were rendering forced tribute to the East India Company. It is significant that the first overt move made against the mother country by the colonists was the dumping of Company tea into Boston Harbor in 1773. Since the right to trade where and with whom they pleased was one of the principles the colonists fought for, it was inevitable, once the war with the English was brought to a close and the new Republic established, that American ships should be directed abroad in search of trade. No ports seemed to offer richer

rewards to the trader than those of the Orient.

The first American vessel to reach Canton, the *Empress of China*, sailed from New York on February 22, 1784, just a month after Congress had ratified the peace treaty with England. On this memorable voyage, with Samuel Shaw of Boston as supercargo, the ship followed the traditional easterly course of the European China Traders around the tip of Africa, arriving at Canton during the summer.

In Samuel Shaw the United States was represented by an able and distinguished citizen (Fig. 18). As his kinsman Josiah Quincy wrote in the Memoir which formed an introduction to *The Journals of Major Samuel Shaw*: "It was his fortune and happiness during his residence in [Canton], by his official influence [on his second trip there he held the purely honorary rank of American Consul], to give to its inhabitants the first impression of the character and the resources of a new nation, of even whose existence the Chinese had previously no knowledge. His intelligence, business talent, and fidelity to his duties and engagements, his amenity of manners and gentlemanly bearing, greatly contributed to establish, in that remote country, confidence and respect for the American people." Unhappily, Shaw did not live to see the full flowering of this new commercial development. He died on shipboard in 1794 while returning from the East at the age of thirty-nine.

In his voyage on the *Empress of China* Shaw represented no established company; in fact, no American company was ever founded to carry on trade with China. In actual practice each American ship had to look out for itself. It could proceed as it wished and make the most, whatever the hazard, of any opportunities coming its way.

The Yankees had few ships and but little capital in the form of specie. And aside from ginseng—an herb that grew wild in American woods, and that was readily sold in China owing to its supposed medicinal properties—they possessed no exportable staples of their own, such as silver, tin, or woolens, to offer to the Chinese. They were, however, able to challenge the su-

FIGURE 18 *Fruit basket and stand decorated with the monogram S.S. of Major Samuel Shaw of Boston and the badge of the Order of the Cincinnati* China-Trade porcelain. About 1786. The Henry Francis duPont Winterthur Museum, Winterthur, Delaware

premacy of the English traders by methods of their own devising.

Their great innovation was the development of intermediate markets, in which the merchant adventurers of Boston played a decisive role. Chief among these markets was the Pacific Northwest coast. At the close of the Revolution that area of the American continent was still virtually unknown. Behind its rugged surf-bordered shores, so dangerously inhospitable to shipping, lived tribes of unfriendly Indians. It was along these shores that the New Englanders found a commodity that they could profitably sell on the Chinese mart, for the coastal waters abounded in fur-bearing creatures, chief of which were the sea otter, with its lustrous pelt, and the seal. Moreover, the Indians were there to hunt them down. Here, indeed, was a rich, virgin field for exploitation. Although the first ships to engage in the fur trade happened to be two of the English East India Company which spent the season of 1787 in that region, it remained for the Americans to explore fully all its possibilities.

In 1788 the first American ship reached the Northwest coast. It was the *Columbia*, which on its voyage from Boston to Canton, instead of taking the normal route past the Cape of Good Hope into the Indian Ocean, sailed westwards around stormy Cape Horn and followed the Pacific coast northwards. On the Northwest coast it acquired a supply of furs which were later profitably disposed of at Canton. On its next voyage, in 1792, it reached the great river, until then unknown, which ever since has been called, in honor of the ship, the Columbia.

In that area north of California a generation of New Englanders engaged in the fur trade with the Indians. The Yankees came to know the region intimately, for it often took a whole year of cruising along the coastline to obtain a full cargo. This undertaking was risky, for the Indians could never be counted on, and bloody skirmishes were frequent. But it was also highly rewarding.

Because of the prices they commanded at Canton, the pelts of the sea otter were most sought after by the traders. They accepted seal-skins also, which were to be had almost for the asking, although these were far less valuable in China. In exchange for the pelts the Yankees traded to the Indians a miscellany of items: blankets, shoes, nails, chisels, gimlets, and beads. In 1790, for instance, two hundred chisels were exchanged for a like number of sea-otter skins. The chisels were of the cheapest sort and could be made right on the ship; the skins brought fifty dollars apiece on the Canton market.

Once the furs were secured, it was the usual thing for ships to proceed to Hawaii, where other commodities, particularly sandalwood, were to be obtained. On a successful trip the profits made by the sale in China of goods acquired on the Northwest coast and in Hawaii could be counted on to defray the entire cost of the venture. As a result, the cargoes that were brought home were sheer profit. The ship *Pearl*, for example, which with its outfit and cargo was valued at not more than $40,000 when it left America, was able in 1810 to purchase more than $150,000 worth of goods in Canton and to bring back to its American owners a clear profit of $200,000.

Merchants not only from Boston but from New York, Providence, and Philadelphia, and from various other ports along the Atlantic seaboard of the United States carried on a regular trade with the East. The greatest number of ships came from New York. For a time Salem on the North Shore of Massachusetts was another center of the China Trade, and fascinating records of that town's activity are still to be found in its Peabody Museum. The ships of Salem generally continued to follow the ancient route by way of the Indian Ocean. On their way to Canton they traded wherever they felt they could do profitable business—in Europe, Africa, South America, India, and the Indies—and they did not disdain to stop for further trading on their long voyages home.

In general, the American ships (Fig. 19) were smaller than the English. At the turn of the century nearly all American vessels were well under 500 tons, whereas those of the English were more than twice that size. On the other hand, the American craft were faster and seem to have been operated more efficiently. For the year 1820, to cite the figures for just one year, the value per ship's ton of the cargoes taken on at Canton was $493 for the Americans as compared to $373 for the English.

It may be pointed out, also, that the masters of the American ships were of a different sort

from those in command of the English ships, often bearing more resemblance to the bold voyagers of the sixteenth and seventeenth centuries than to the well-schooled Englishmen of the eighteenth century. Consider, for example, the *Union*, commanded by John Boit, Jr.—a lad of nineteen years—which sailed from Boston on August 1, 1794. The *Union*, an 89-ton sloop, measured sixty feet in length and carried a crew of twenty-two. It rounded the Horn, traded on the Northwest coast and at Canton, and returned safely to home port on July 8, 1796, having circumnavigated the globe in less than two years. On this feat Samuel Eliot Morison commented in his *Maritime History of Massachusetts*:

In view of the newspaper publicity given nowadays to men of twice Boit's age and experience for crossing the Atlantic in vessels no smaller than the *Union* and far better equipped, it is refreshing to note the scant attention he got. "Sloop Union, Boit, Canton," in small type at the end of 'Arrivals' in the "Boston Centinel." That was all!

Using such methods and directed by such men, the Yankee trade grew by leaps and bounds. The English showed signs of discomfiture on the American success. In 1793, a year

FIGURE 19 *The sloop* Union *returning to Boston from Canton, 1796*

Water color by Captain John Boit illustrating his "Journal of the Voyage . . ." Massachusetts Historical Society, Boston

when six American vessels were anchored off Whampoa, Lord Macartney, who was then in Canton on his ambassadorial mission, felt constrained to ask the Viceroy, among other things, "that the English not be confounded with other persons who trade to Canton and speak the same Language, but [are of] a different nation, and inhabit a very different part of the world called America."

The English had good reason to fear this new rival, whose increasing share in the China Trade was rapidly becoming a serious threat to their interests. They who for a century had been cocks of the walk among Westerners in Canton now found themselves unable to meet the Yankee challenge. After 1800 an average of more than thirty American ships annually were to be found in Canton. The effectiveness of the American methods was surely a factor contributing to the decision in 1834, during the final days of the old China Trade, to dissolve the English Company.

[6]

To the Chinese all foreigners trading in Canton were Fan Kwaes—foreign devils. And like devils, reasoned the Chinese, they needed the closest watching. These devils, though, were not all one kind. The English were the "Red-haired" devils, and the Parsees from India, who shaved their heads, were the "White-haired" devils. The French were "Fat-lan-sy"; the Dutch, "Ho-lan" (they were also called "Red-haired" devils); the Swedes, "Suy"; the Danes, "Yellow-flag" devils; and the Portuguese, "Se-yang Kwae," devils of the Western Ocean. The Americans were the "Flowery-flag" devils.

In order to supervise these "devils" the Chinese required that, under the law, each one put himself into the hands of one of a small number of Chinese known as Guild, or Hong, Merchants. With minor exceptions, all business dealings had to be undertaken through this merchant.

The foreigner was free only to select the particular merchant with whom he would deal. Thereafter he was entirely in the hands of the Oriental, who was known as his "Security Merchant" and who was responsible for all his trade. He had to sell his imports at prices set by the Security Merchant. He could deal with no other Cantonese. He then had to buy all his return cargo from this same individual, and again at the latter's price. All arrangements having to do with the ship's stay in Canton came under the watchful eyes of this Chinese. The Security Merchant also leased the Companies their factory buildings; he paid all duties on merchandise purchased; he was go-between in all disputes involving Europeans and Chinese authorities. The Chinese government even held him responsible for the individual and collective good conduct of factory personnel and crew members.

The Security Merchant was China's answer to the threat posed by the supercargo, the foreign leader in the mercantile siege of that nation. It is no coincidence that the Guild of Merchants was established by Imperial edict in 1720, only five years after the creation of the English East India Company factory at Canton. In 1755 that monopoly was reaffirmed under the name of Hong Merchants. Altogether, about a dozen merchants were included in that select group. To give these men absolute control over the China Trade, the Emperor Ch'ien Lung decreed in 1757 that no port of China, save Canton, would thereafter be open to Western shipping, thus giving Imperial confirmation to a ruling long in force.

As the supercargo was responsible to his Company, the Guild or Hong Merchant was responsible to his government. Although he could, if he were shrewd and lucky, amass a fortune, his lot was far from enviable. China was not a capitalist country, and the merchant class was completely without rank or power, its every move being subject to the dictate of the officeholding mandarins. The Merchant Guild actually existed as a convenient tool by means of which government officials could profit from the foreign trade they themselves professed to despise. Riding on each merchant's shoulders, therefore, was a flock of officeholders, from the Viceroy of the Province of Canton down to the most miserable, petty official penny-grabber, each demanding a share in the proceeds. Even the exceptional Houqua (Fig. 20), who in the late years of the old China Trade managed to become in the eyes of the Westerners a merchant prince with an estimated capital in 1834 of $26,000,000, was said to be spineless when dealing with his own government's officials. Under such a system many a merchant went bankrupt.

But the virtue of the Chinese method of managing the foreign trade was that it worked. As Morse has noted:

The best commentary on the commercial aspect of the system is the admitted fact that there grew up side by side, during a century of joint working, a body of Chinese and of foreign merchants, than whom there has never, at any time, or at any place, been a more honourable; with never a written contract, with many an occasion of help in time of difficulty, and with much sympathy and friendliness from the one to the other. And yet, all this was paid for by the foreign traders.

The traders paid for it and liked it not. They simply had to put up with it. Throughout the eighteenth century, however, the English continually asked for relief from regulations which were ever of a more restrictive nature. Most galling to them, perhaps, was their forced segregation within the narrow limits of the factory area, where they lived as in a prison camp. Yet in all their protestations they got nowhere; if anything, the lot of the Westerners worsened.

Never did they have official representatives of their own upon whom they could rely for help, for China haughtily disdained to "recognize" any European country as either friend or foe. At one juncture, in 1793, the British government sent an ambassadorial mission headed by Lord Macartney to the Emperor Ch'ien Lung to ask for a revision of conditions so that the English traders might live and work in a manner compatible with the dignity of their nation. On the way to interview the Emperor, Macartney's entourage was preceded by Chinese bearing banners on which were inscribed the words "Tribute Bearers." The Emperor Ch'ien Lung's

FIGURE 20   *Houqua, the senior Hong Merchant of Canton*

Chinese copy after a painting by George Chinnery. About 1825. The Metropolitan Museum of Art

condescending answer to the petition is summed up in these words from his letter to King George III of England: "As the Requests made by your Ambassador militate against the Laws and Usages of this Our Empire, and are at the same Time wholly useless to the End proposed, I cannot acquiesce in them. I again admonish you, O King, to act conformably to my Intentions . . ."

Ch'ien Lung was at that time able to call the tune and so, for a while, were his successors. Western pressure on China, however, was intensifying as ever more ships came to trade there, and finally in the 1830s it was to explode through all the mandarinic paper barriers set up to restrain it. That, however, goes beyond the limits of our narrative, which is primarily concerned with the eighteenth century, the great era of the porcelain trade.

THE TRADE IN PORCELAIN

The importation to the West of the finest of the China-Trade porcelain was a long and complicated process. The starting point was probably a quiet London shop or office as remote in distance from the source of the product as was the time of the placement of the order from its completion—at least two years.

This was not true, of course, of the ordinary porcelain, such as the blue-and-white wares or undecorated white dishes which received their enamel ornament in Europe. These dishes were easy to get in Canton by the thousand, and when consignments arrived in London they were usually put up at public auction. Shipments by the English Company were sold in this manner at East India House in Leadenhall Street.

But it was a far different matter when it came to filling special orders. Instructions for the decoration of armorial ware of the type forming the bulk of the McCann collection had of necessity to originate in the West. Though evidence on the matter is wanting, we may assume that porcelains of this sort destined for English customers were ordered in London either directly through the East India Company or through certain shopkeepers.

There was a considerable number of London merchants, or "chinamen" as they were called, who specialized in the sale of Oriental goods (Fig. 21). It has been noted that in the London Directories for the year 1774 no less than fifty-two such merchants were listed. It is reasonable to suppose that these shopkeepers accepted orders for specially decorated porcelain services, although there is no evidence to give direct support to such a belief or to indicate how transactions of this sort might have been carried out. We may presume, however, that in a shop of this character—as in the East India Company office—a customer could decide upon the type of service he required. In placing his order, he would surely leave specific directions for the painting of the armorial decorations, furnishing an exact drawing with notes of the colors to be used. To assist in the choice and designation of borders, an ingenious arrangement was devised sometime around the last quarter of the century. Sample plates manufactured in China were dispatched to Europe in what were called "Pattern Chests." Sample plates, now extremely rare, are readily recognizable, for their border decoration is quartered, each quarter showing a different pattern (Fig. 22). On a sample plate in the Victoria and Albert Museum the individual patterns are numbered in enameled arabic figures. These numbers are said to indicate where the prices would be found in an accompanying catalogue.

It is to be presumed that when an order had been given, the shopkeeper would commission a supercargo or ship's officer about to leave for China to execute it as part of his private trade. Upon the arrival of that official in Canton many months later, the order would be placed in the hands of one of the local shopmen. The English Company ships were usually laid up for at least three months at the Whampoa anchorage. Usually the purchaser in England had to wait no less than two years for notification that his porcelain had arrived and was ready for him in the London shop where his order had been placed.

[2]

Although in negotiating for tea and silk the foreign traders at Canton had to deal exclusively through their Security Merchants, in porcelain there was a relatively free market. Official Company orders for porcelain had to be filled by the proper Security Merchants, but in private trade supercargoes and ships' officers were permitted to deal directly with any of the small shopmen whose stores lined the streets and alleys of the foreign-factory area.

Private trade had been sanctioned by general agreement since first the Westerners began dealing with the Cantonese. When the Merchants' Guild was founded in 1720, among the articles of its Charter, which otherwise restricted all foreign trade to Guild members, was one which read: "Chinaware requiring technical knowledge . . . [is] left free to all . . ."

The purchasing of porcelain indeed required

"technical knowledge," for the material varied greatly as to quality, size, shape, and decoration. It was a knowledge easily acquired by the Chinese, who were thoroughly familiar with porcelain. In time, also, a certain expertness was acquired by various Europeans. In 1734, for example, a Mr. John Scrivener, who must be set down as the first recognized Western expert in Chinese porcelain, was sent to Canton on the *Harrison* as being "one 'having Judgment in Tea & Chinaware.'" According to Hosea Ballou Morse, "his opinion on tea was sometimes accepted by the supercargoes and sometimes not; but on chinaware it was listened to with respect."

In the course of time the Merchants' Guild, jealous of any and all competition, eventually

FIGURE 21 *Trade card of John Dobson*

Dobson, one of the numerous "chinamen" in mid-XVIII-century London, sold Oriental porcelains at his shop "at the China Jarr." The Metropolitan Museum of Art

FIGURE 22 *Sample plates for China-Trade porcelain. 1790–1800*

Plate above, Göteborgs Historiska Museum, Göteborg, Sweden. Plate below, Victoria and Albert Museum, London

tion which, besides giving an indication of the deep rivalry existing between the two groups of Chinese merchants, records the number of small shops in the factory area and the character of their proprietors. After stating that dealings with the various East India Companies were the sole province of the Merchants' Guild, the proclamation went on as follows: ". . . we find by Enquiry that the Number of Shops in Canton amount to one hundred and upwards, and although amongst these petty dealers there are some of no Considerable Substance, yet they understand the language of the Foreigners and have small Capitals [*sic*]. To prohibit all of them from dealing with the Europeans would neither be conformable to reason nor to the Regard we entertain for the public Good." The shopmen were thereupon ordered to divide themselves into groups of five, each of which would be under the responsible supervision of one of the Guild Merchants, "which being done they shall be permitted to carry on a Retail Trade with the Foreigners, and also to deal with them for their private Merchandise."

The interior of one of the hundred-odd shops frequented by Europeans is depicted in a sketch owned by the British Museum (Fig. 23). Another is shown on a cup and saucer of 1725–1740 in the McCann collection (Frontispiece). On the saucer we are given a picture of a shop's arrangement, its simple shelves and counters recalling typical stores of the Chinese districts in some of the larger Western cities. The shelves of the shop are lined with porcelains, and among the Chinese clerks are Europeans wearing what a Chinese porcelain painter conceived as Occidental clothing. On the side of the teacup is another entertaining scene in which a transaction is being carried on between a Chinese and two wide-eyed European clients.

[3]

Once the order was given to a shopman in Canton it was sent along to one of the local establishments where porcelains received their final decoration. These places seem to have kept on hand a large stock of undecorated or par-

secured an effective control over the shopmen. In 1755 the Hong Merchants petitioned their government that the activities of the shopmen be strictly limited and subject to their direction. In supporting these requests the Viceroy and the Hoppo (customs official) issued a proclama-

tially decorated porcelain sent from Ching-techen. With such an arrangement it was generally possible to fill immediately whatever order was received for the decoration of porcelain to Western specification.

All the establishments in which the chinaware was given its final decoration were located in the suburbs of Canton. The progress of the work could therefore be watched and directed by the merchants who were actually dealing with the European agents. Some of the workshops were in the immediate vicinity of the East India Company factories. In his *Memoirs* William Hickey described a tour of a number of these workshops which he made with two Company officials in 1769. "We were then shewn the different processes used in finishing the China ware. In one long gallery we found upwards of a hundred persons at work in sketching or finishing the various ornaments upon each particular piece of the ware, some parts being executed by men of a very advanced age, others by children even so young as six or seven years . . ."

Other establishments were located directly across the river from Canton on the island of Honan, where the Pleasure Gardens were located to which the Chinese admitted Europeans three times a month—and no more—on the eighth day, the eighteenth, and the twenty-eighth. Father du Halde stated that there were still other establishments in the borough of Fo-shan, a few miles upstream from Canton. "Tho' the Number of Artificers in this City is almost incredible," he wrote, "yet not being sufficient for its Trade, they have establish'd a great many Manufactories at *Fo-shan*, which has render'd it famous thro' the whole Province."

William Hickey's description of both the very aged and the very young at work decorating porcelains suggests that the Cantonese factories practiced the same division of labor which Father d'Entrecolles had noted at Chingtechen. In no way except by such a system can the standardized products of Canton be fully accounted for. It was, moreover, a manner of working which seemingly fitted the temperament of the Cantonese workers, who are described by

Father du Halde as "very industrious, and tho' not quick at Invention, they are very expert at imitating any sort of *European* Work that is shown them, and immediately make such another in great Perfection." They were, in short, facile and uninspired.

The unimaginative fidelity of the Cantonese craftsmen has been widely commented on by students of porcelain. It is especially evident in the painting of the armorial decorations sent them from Europe, an occupation in which exactitude was necessary both in line and in color. As might be expected, mistakes did sometimes creep in. In *The Book of Famille Rose*, G. C. Williamson reported that such inscriptions as "Copy these arms exactly," and "This is the Drawing to copy," have been found on porcelains painted by Chinese who, in their ignorance of the English language, copied both the model and the accompanying directions. And Cosmo Monkhouse described still another of these errors in his work *Chinese Porcelain*:

In my possession is a plate presented to me by a friend who is the living representative of the old Guernsey family of Andros, which offers an amusing instance of Chinese fidelity in imitation. The family ordered a service to be painted with their arms, and for the guidance of the artist sent a pen or pencil

FIGURE 23 *Interior of a Cantonese porcelain shop*

Drawing in ink made in Canton for the European market. British Museum

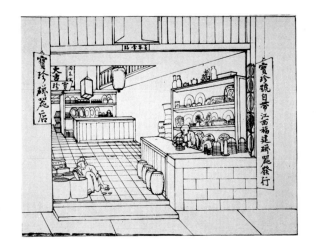

drawing of them with the name of each colour written in the appropriate compartment. The service returned duly painted, but the artist took the words "red," "green," "blue," to be part of the decoration, and copied them exactly as written. There they are still to be observed under the enamel, which is never of the right colour. Thus, under the red is the word "blue," and *vice versâ.* The family then ordered another service, taking the precaution to send out a drawing of their arms carefully emblazoned in the right colours. I have also a plate of the second service, which was quite successful.

Despite these occasional lapses, the Cantonese craftsmen were generally able to fill European orders quickly, accurately, and successfully.

The Chinese themselves did not have a high opinion of Cantonese craftsmanship in general. Du Halde noted that the various manufactures of that city "are not much esteem'd at *Pe-king,* because the Workmen there undervalue them, as being neither substantial nor well wrought; for generally the Materials they are made of, are too scanty or ill chosen, or else the Workmanship within is too slight." With respect to porcelain, the refinements required by the educated Chinese, fully aware of all the subtle values that go to make a first-rate piece, were neither necessary nor practical for the large-scale activities of the Canton trade. And there can be no question but that the Cantonese were well equipped to meet the special but less exacting demands of the European market. Producing for export was their chief concern, for they had been engaged long before the arrival of the Europeans in procuring and manufacturing commodities for various Asiatic countries.

[4]

Though the quality of the painted porcelain was not always high in the eyes of the Chinese, the prices were satisfyingly low from the Western point of view. A two-gallon punch bowl, for example, cost 4 shillings and 8 pence. Single blue-and-white plates were $2\frac{2}{3}$ pennies each, and teacups and saucers cost according to the size of the porcelains from 2 pennies to $3\frac{1}{3}$ pennies the

pair. These were Canton prices for wares ordered in wholesale lots in 1772. Even if a markup of 100 per cent be envisaged for freight charges and profits, the retail prices in Europe would still be low by Western standards.

The cheapness of porcelain is implicit in the story of young Bob Potts, an apprentice attached to the English East India Company factory at Canton in 1769. Potts was a high-spirited lad of fourteen with seemingly little to do except make mischief. His friend William Hickey related an incident concerning him in his *Memoirs*:

[Potts] passed most of his time in our rooms [in the Factory] . . . He breakfasted with us, and, if he took it into his head that McClintock was too long at the meal, or drank too much tea, he, without the least ceremony, overset the table. The first time he practised this, I was very angry at such a quantity of handsome china being thus mischievously demolished, and expressed my displeasure thereat, which

FIGURE 24

Invoice for a service of chinaware made for Charles Peers, dated Canton, December 10, 1731. British Museum

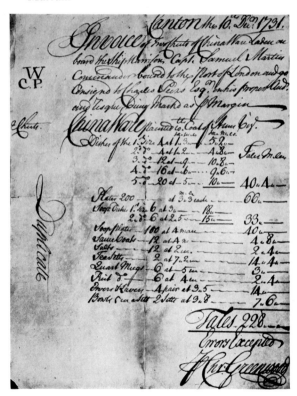

only excited the mirth of the young pickle. "Why, Zounds!" said he, "you surely forget where you are. I never suffer the servants to have the trouble of removing a tea equipage, always throwing the whole apparatus out of window or downstairs. They easily procure another batch from the steward's warehouse."

There was something to be said for such a system. If the broken porcelains were the ordinary blue-and-white wares, as surely they were, the cost to the Company each time Potts went into action would have amounted to less than a shilling at the very most.

The prices so far mentioned refer to the commoner wares. Fortunately, a few documents also exist relating to the prices of porcelains made to special order, and these round out our story of the price aspect of the porcelain trade. Two detailed invoices for wares painted in Canton are in the British Museum. One of them (Fig. 24), dated 1731, is for a service made for Charles Peers. Since the British Museum also possesses two plates from the Peers service, the invoice is more than usually enlightening. Representing the consistently dependable standard of Cantonese workmanship, the Peers plate here illustrated (Fig. 25) is decorated with floral borders characteristic of the China-Trade ware of the period and with the coat of arms of the family.

There were about 500 pieces in the entire service, and the total price was £76 (228 taels). It is difficult to determine exactly the purchasing power of the English pound in 1731. On the other hand, it seems more than evident that £76 was a reasonable figure for such a service. It would, of course, be helpful to compare the price with sums paid for comparable European services. But at the time when the Peers service was made no porcelain service had yet been produced in Europe. The first large Meissen service, made for Count Hennicke, dates from 1735 and was, presumably, very costly. And it seems doubtful whether any of the porcelain services made in Europe later in the eighteenth century could compete in price with comparable Cantonese wares. Price, as well as the desire for services and the admiration for porcelain as a

FIGURE 25

Plate from the Peers service. China-Trade porcelain made for the English market in 1731. British Museum

material, was a factor that contributed largely to the sensational growth of the trade.

The Peers invoice is of further significance for our study in that it gives us a basis for comparing the prices of the Canton-decorated pieces with the more common blue-and-white wares of the China Trade. Take, for example, the Peers plates. Each cost a fraction over 2 shillings. A blue-and-white plate, as we have seen, fetched $2\frac{2}{3}$ pennies at Canton. Even when allowance is made for the somewhat higher prices paid for the latter when retailed in Europe, the difference in cost for the two types of ware is that between shillings and pennies. This being the case, the armorial porcelains and the other pieces so carefully decorated at Canton were hardly of the sort to be tossed casually out of windows.

[5]

Our interest in the China Trade centers upon porcelain. Yet porcelain was actually no more than a stepchild of that famous trade. Despite the amount of porcelain it carried during the eighteenth century, the English Company, which was the chief exporter of the material and which may be taken as an exemplar for all European East India Companies, was not particularly interested in the material. The Company's preoccupation was tea. Raw silk came next. Both brought gratifyingly high profits. Porcelain was considered a minor, although welcome, addition to the export list. It is true that there was a ready and reasonably profitable market for porcelain in England. But one of its chief virtues, as the Company saw it, was the highly useful role it played as ballast in the proper handling of the ship's cargo.

Until the year 1772 the registered weight of Company ships was almost invariably 499 tons, and this for a curious reason: by English law any vessel above that weight was required to have a chaplain aboard. It was only in the nineteenth century that great 1,000-ton Company ships plowed the Eastern seas. Space was therefore understandably at a premium. Thanks,

FIGURE 26 *Workmen in a Cantonese factory packing porcelain for shipment abroad*

Chinese painting. Probably late XVIII century. British Museum

however, to its dead weight, a well-packed chest containing as many as 600 pieces of porcelain and weighing approximately 500 pounds was the equivalent of a chest of bricks and formed excellent ballast. Hence it came about that the hold was ordinarily floored with chests of porcelain. Upon this flooring were placed the chests of tea, first the teas of lesser quality and then, at a higher level, the finer grades. Resting on top of the teas were the chests and bales of woven and raw silk, the commodity most susceptible to damage.

Some of the porcelain stowed away in this manner represented official Company shipments; some of it, as has been indicated, was part of the private trade sent home by supercargoes and officers of the Company ships as a share of their reward in the venture. Although Company officials were never allowed to export on their own more than an insignificant amount of tea, the rules were relaxed with regard to porcelain. In 1771, to cite one typical example, the Commander of the *Cruttenden*, one of the ships then in Canton, brought back on his own 116 chests of the ware. The amount of porcelain

permitted for private trade by supercargoes and ships' officers varied through the years; at one point the maximum value allowed was £2,500.

The East India Company records for the quantities of tea and silk shipped out of Canton are fairly complete; but this is far from the case with porcelain, partly, no doubt, because so much of it figured as private trade.

The Company records present a general picture of the porcelain trade in the eighteenth century through the documentation of quantity shipments (Fig. 26). The figures they offer, usually for shipments of undecorated and blue-and-white wares, give us the broad economic background of the commerce in porcelain against which the more specialized trade with which we are concerned may be effectively silhouetted. We discover, for example, that in 1753 five trading vessels—two of them English, the others flying the flags of France, Holland, and Denmark—carried to Europe an estimated million pieces of chinaware. In 1772 the English Company alone placed advance orders for delivery the following year of about 400,000 pieces. Almost all of these may be presumed to have been the inexpensive wares of Chingtechen, for whenever their color is indicated, it is always "blue and white."

For indications of the commerce in armorial and other specially decorated porcelain sent to Europe, we look for evidence outside the Company records. Such evidence is to be found in Sir Algernon Tudor-Craig's study *Armorial Porcelain*, in which examples of more than 1,200 different services are listed and are given approximate dates on the basis of their designs and their histories.

The Tudor-Craig list may be summarized as follows:

YEARS	NUMBER OF SERVICES
1700–1710	None
1710–1720	19
1720–1730	96
1730–1740	114
1740–1750	192
1750–1760	299
1760–1770	145

YEARS	NUMBER OF SERVICES
1770–1780	159
1780–1790	144
1790–1800	95
1800–1810	9
1810–1820	3

This list bears directly on the armorial porcelains decorated at Canton, so richly represented in the McCann collection. It charts the steady growth of this aspect of the porcelain trade during the first half of the eighteenth century, its high point at the middle of the century, and its gradual decline until, by the early decades of the nineteenth century, the amount exported had become negligible.

The development it traces is in line with other events, especially with two that marked the effective beginnings and, as far as England was concerned, the virtual termination of the porcelain trade. One was the establishment of the English factory at Canton in 1715; the other was the decision taken by the directors of the English East India Company in 1801 to exclude porcelain as part of their ships' regular cargoes. This decision, it may be noted, seems to have been due to a variety of causes—to changes of fashion (things Chinese were losing their appeal), to the rise of the European ceramic industry to the point where it could supply cheaply and well all demands made upon it, and to the imposition of tariff walls as a protection to that industry.

Although by the beginning of the nineteenth century European imports of China-Trade ware almost ceased, it is of interest to note that a considerable amount of porcelain, especially that decorated in underglaze colors at Chingtechen, was dispatched to the United States during the first half of the nineteenth century. American ships, it will be remembered, were late arrivals at Canton. Also there were no established manufactories of ceramic wares in the United States that could offer competition to the Chinese imports. Not until the 1820s were the export wares of China challenged on the American market, and then successfully by the mass-produced potteries of Staffordshire.

CHINA IN EUROPE

We have by now seen something of the history of China-Trade porcelain, that variety of Chinese porcelain that was destined for the West. We have followed the course of the manufacture of the material from Chingtechen to Canton, where some of the porcelain received its final decorations and where all of it was prepared for ocean shipment. Finally, we have described the trade in porcelain as part of a globe-girdling commerce and the role of the East India Companies, representatives of the West, in furthering it.

But how was porcelain received in the lands of the West? Indeed, what did the peoples of the West know about it—or of the region from which it came and of the Chinese who created it? How was porcelain to fit in with the art of the West and what, if any, influence was it to have on media and styles of Western art?

At first porcelain was one of the rarest of commodities, a precious substance, commanding the admiration of emperors and kings. Before the sea lanes to the East were opened in the sixteenth century, only an occasional piece found its way to the West by overland caravan routes. But even in the sixteenth century, after the opening of communication with the Orient by sea, it remained a great rarity. In 1587 Lord Burghley chose a piece of porcelain as a New Year's present for his sovereign, Queen Elizabeth. At the very end of the sixteenth century a French writer, Loys Guyon, had this to say of porcelain's proud estate: "Great value is attached to [porcelain], and it is highly esteemed among princes, both heathen and Christian. This is so true that the most expensive and rare salads, fruits, and preserves count for nothing if they are not served in porcelain. Only thus is the table honored. Popes, kings, emperors, dukes, Italian marquises, and, above all, emperors and dukes, follow this custom."

This eager acceptance of porcelain in royal circles in the sixteenth and seventeenth centuries set the stage for its later success with the generality of the people in the eighteenth. Instances of royal or near-royal use abound in the earlier period. As a child, for example, Louis XIII of

France took his bouillon from a porcelain écuelle. And in 1649 porcelain was listed in the inventory of the collection formed by the greatest connoisseur of France, Cardinal Mazarin. In a rhymed description of a famous banquet which the Cardinal gave in 1653, Mlle de Montpensier included the following couplet:

En plats d'argent et porcelaine
Traita le Roy et les deux Reines.

During the second half of the century, in the reign of Louis XIV, there were ever more references to the material. The king himself, who, like his predecessor, drank bouillon from a porcelain vessel, on one occasion purchased over 9,000 livres worth of porcelain. His favorite, Madame de Maintenon, had a mantelpiece in her apartment at Saint-Cyr decorated with 182 small porcelains which came to her as a gift from the monarch and which previously had come to him as a gift from the King of Siam. A verse written in 1716—just when Westerners started trading at Canton—sums up the prevailing French attitude towards the material:

Allons à cette porcelaine,
Sa beauté m'invite, m'entraîne,
Elle vient du monde nouveau,
L'on ne peut rien voir de plus beau.
Qu'elle a d'attrait et qu'elle est fine!
Elle est native de la Chine.

"Let us," the poet rhapsodized, "rush to this porcelain. Its beauty entices me, and sends me into transports. It comes from a new world; nothing more fair can be seen. How attractive it is, how very fine. China is the land of its birth."

[2]

Chinese porcelain's success in Europe of the eighteenth century was not due solely to the novelty and charm of the material. After a long past of general ignorance of the Far East, in the seventeenth century Europeans had suddenly become aware of the existence of China, a vast and remote state possessed of a culture and tradition that rivaled their own. They were entranced with what they found. Everything Chinese seemed good to them: Chinese religion, law, manners, customs—and all the things the Chinese made.

Knowledge of China came to the West by various means. The porcelains, silks, lacquers, and other commodities which were brought to Europe as part of the commerce with the Orient offered impressive testimony of the high state of Chinese civilization. Further evidence came from the reports of Western traders. Together, however, these two could do no more than give a fragmentary picture of the land, for the Oriental goods were divorced from their normal settings, and the traders' reports were all made by men who had never actually gained access into China proper.

Europeans received their most detailed and accurate picture from still another source, the early Jesuit missionaries to China. At first, like all other Westerners, the Jesuits were barred from China proper. Finally, late in the sixteenth century, Father Matteo Ricci (see Fig. 27), who with his companions had been for years hopefully working at Macao, succeeded in gaining entry.

Ricci succeeded because he was a man of wide learning, able thereby to win the esteem of a number of the Chinese scholars. Because he was an intellectual, ways were opened to him that would always be closed to Western merchants, engaged as they were in trade, an occupation which the mandarins—members of the scholar class which occupied all leading government posts—believed to be demeaning. Ricci even wore the robes of a mandarin and let his beard grow in the manner of a Chinese scholar. By the beginning of the seventeenth century he was allowed to live in Peking, where the same qualities of mind that had impressed Chinese scholars won him favor with the Emperor. Through Ricci's efforts a small number of Jesuits were enabled to enter China. As he lay dying, in 1610, he told them: "I am leaving you on the threshold of an open door."

43

From the first the aim of the Jesuits was to "keep the door open." Under the leadership of men like Fathers Schaal and Verbiest (see Fig. 27), they did so simply by making themselves so useful that a succession of emperors came to depend on them for a variety of services. Some of the priests who were expert mathematicians and astronomers reformed the calendar, a task of major importance to the Chinese. Others with gifts for diplomacy advised on questions of foreign affairs. Some cast ordnance for the Chinese army. Others engaged in map making.

Through their formal writings and their letters the missionaries also endeavored to make China known to the West and to relate what they saw in the Orient to Western experience. They proved on the whole to be excellent reporters of the China scene. They were curious, observant, and concerned with all aspects of life. Since they were optimistic for China's eventual conversion and sought to gain support in Europe for their work, they tended to favor the land they hoped one day to win. So it was that the picture of China as given to the West

had a utopian glow. Few there were who failed to succumb to its enchantment.

Among the many Jesuit books dealing with various aspects of Chinese life and culture, the titles of a few may be noted. Father Kircher's *China illustrata* (1667), with its many engraved plates, was a popular work which immediately captured the fancy of the West. Father Le Compte's *Nouveaux Mémoires sur l'état présent de la Chine*, published in three volumes between 1696 and 1701, was a commentary on Chinese life of the day. The most complete picture of the country as a whole appeared in Father du Halde's *Description . . . de la Chine* (1735). The text was accompanied by maps engraved by D'Anville in Paris after those made by the Jesuits at the command of the Emperor K'anghsi in 1710. *Lettres édifiantes et curieuses écrites des Missions Étrangères*, collections of Jesuit letters published between 1702 and 1776, also added a wealth of detailed information to the China story. The best description of the manufacture of porcelain, as we have already seen, comes from two of these letters, written by Father d'Entrecolles and extensively used by Du Halde. By the middle of the eighteenth century, largely as the result of Jesuit enterprise, Voltaire could assert that China was probably "better known than some of the provinces of Europe."

One of the chief reasons for the great interest in China and for the ready acceptance of things

FIGURE 27 *Father Ricci, Father Schaal, and Father Verbiest, three of the leaders of the Jesuit Mission to China*

Engraving reproduced from Du Halde, *Description . . . de la Chine . . .* , Paris, 1735

Le Pere Matthieu Ricci.   Le Pere Adam Schaal.   Le Pere Ferdinand Verbiest.

MONSEIGNEUR LE DAUPHIN LABOURANT.

O Terre! ouvre ton sein: l'utile agriculture
l'objet de nos dedains s'annoblit en ce jour

l'humanité sourit, et toute la Nature
en voyant travailler l'objet de notre amour.

FIGURE 28 *Louis XVI as Dauphin observing an old Chinese custom, the Festival of the Spring Planting*

Engraving by Michael Wachsmut. French, 1760–1770. The Metropolitan Museum of Art

Chinese was the spirit of reform that was in the air in Europe in the late seventeenth century, a spirit that would grow with the passing decades. The parochial despotism and entrenched conservatism of Church and State were beginning to pall on the more "enlightened" individuals. To such men, who were disenchanted with the all-too-familiar state of things at home, distant China offered what seemed to be an ideal system, one based on an elevated code of ethics "drawn from the finest sources of natural reason," a spirit of tolerance, and a harmonious relationship between all the people joined in a vast family-like group and led by sage and noble rulers.

A number of the wisest men of Europe became propagandists of the Chinese way of life. One of the greatest of Sinophiles was the German philosopher Leibnitz, whose *Novissima Sinica*, published in 1697, was largely based on material that he, a Protestant, had found in Jesuit publications and had supplemented by lengthy correspondence with a number of the Fathers. On one occasion Leibnitz wrote: "I almost think it necessary that Chinese missionaries should be sent to us to teach us the aim and practice of natural theology, as we send missionaries to them to instruct them in revealed theology."

The great French apologists for China were

45

nearly all men of the eighteenth century. Chief among them were the Encyclopedists, and of this group none was more effective than Voltaire, one of whose great stage successes, *L'Orphelin de la Chine* (1755), or "Confucian morals in five acts," as he himself referred to it, was based on a Chinese play, *The Orphan of the House of Chau*, which had appeared in French in 1735 in Du Halde's *Description . . . de la Chine*.

Under such sponsorship, the ethics and law of China became the gospel of the Age of Enlightenment, Confucius became its patron saint, and the average Chinese the symbol of the "virtuous man." The Deists, who saw God with a new vision, that of common sense, and stripped of all mystery, found solid comfort in the moral philosophy of Confucius. Those interested in buttressing the French government, then showing marked signs of decay, saw in the monolithic Chinese system the perfect example of what might be achieved in their own country. The Physiocrats, who aimed at economic reform through the increase and the circulation of wealth derived from agriculture, were equally influenced by the Chinese example (Fig. 28). One of the Physiocrats, Pierre Poivre, wrote in 1769: "China offers an enchanting picture of what the whole world might become, if the laws of that empire were to become the laws of all nations." Poivre then exhorted his readers: "Go to Peking. Gaze upon the mightiest of mortals; he is the true and perfect image of Heaven."

For a variety of reasons the last decades of the eighteenth century saw a speedy decline of European interest in the Orient. For one thing, the times were changing. Ancient Rome, for a while partially eclipsed by the fame of China and other centers, was once more becoming a source of inspiration for the West. China, moreover, was at last being subjected to an unsentimental study by European writers, and as fact was disentangled from fancy a less glamorous picture of that nation was presented. Also, the last decades of the century witnessed a steadily increasing trade with China in the staples of that country, and the significant reports arriving from the East were statistical and

FIGURE 29 *Chinese pagoda in Kew Gardens, London, built by William Chambers in 1761–1762*

46

economic, the work of merchants whose interests lay in the profit side of the ledger. In the light of this new realism, China lost much of her capacity to inspire, to stimulate, and to entertain.

[3]

The impact of Oriental art upon that of the West was not to be long lasting, despite the wide popularity of China and things Chinese during the eighteenth century. By and large, the Oriental forms to be found in Occidental art of that period were no more than ephemeral additions to a style that in its own right was vital and self-contained. A vogue, if it is no more than just that, is apt quickly to be forgotten in favor of the next one to come along. The vogue for China is a case in point. Nevertheless, the fact that the rage for things Chinese was a passing one in Western art is not to say that it had little meaning for the age that surrendered itself so wholeheartedly to it.

The prevailing style of that age was, of course, the rococo, which, as Fiske Kimball pointed out in *The Creation of the Rococo*, was one of the major manifestations of European art. It followed on the heels of the baroque, first coming into existence at the end of the seventeenth century; by the 1760s it was already on the wane in France, although it lingered somewhat longer elsewhere on the Continent. Its full flowering occurred during the reign of Louis XV (1723-1774).

In France, the country of its birth and development, the rococo meant a period of relaxation from the pompous academism known as the *style Louis XIV*. It centered not so much in painting and sculpture as in architecture and the allied decorative arts. Basically, the rococo represented an ornamental style and its application to all the arts of decoration. The creators of the rococo worked in a spirit of genial fantasy. When it served their purpose realism, and its mainstay in Western art, perspective, were disregarded. By such means they produced a fresh and informal style thoroughly in harmony with the relaxed state of French society at the moment.

During the relatively brief period of the rococo, Chinese forms became widely used in European art. It was a coincidence, and a happy one for Europe, that at the moment of rococo's ascendancy China possessed a style in many ways similar to it. Like France, China of the eighteenth century also experienced a period of relaxation from the tensions and pretensions of the immediate past. The period of Ch'ien Lung had much in common with that of his contemporary, Louis XV. It was an age less celebrated for its painting and sculpture than for its works in the decorative arts—especially porcelain. In such productions fantasy had the freest sort of play. Geometric perspective had, of course, never counted in the Orient. The light touch was definitely preferred, and asymmetry was the order of the day.

Quite by accident, then, there was for a brief period in the field of applied art a common meeting ground for East and West. But the two cultures met as strangers, and when late in the century they parted company, they were strangers still.

During this period, however, the style known as "chinoiserie" came into being and flourished. The word chinoiserie, which describes those works of European art in which Chinese elements are used, evokes a host of images at once exotic, delightful, and surprising. Examples of this style may actually be found in pre-rococo France, one of the earliest being the Trianon de porcelaine, a garden casino which once existed at Versailles. It was made at the order of Louis XIV before 1670 and was decorated with figures painted in blue "in the manner of works coming from China."

It was in such informal pavilions placed in garden settings that chinoiserie achieved some of its most startling effects. Especially was this the case in Germany where chinoiserie and rococo, to which chinoiserie quickly became allied, were eventually found in their most uninhibited forms. Augustus the Strong of Saxony erected a Japanese Palace in Dresden between 1715 and 1717. In 1719 Max Emanuel constructed for the park at Nymphenburg, on the

FIGURE 30

Chinoiserie ornament print by Gabriel Huquier. French, about 1735. The Albertina, Vienna

outskirts of Munich, the famous Pagoda Tower, largely painted in blue with Chinese decorations in imitation of the Trianon de porcelaine. And the Japanese pavilion at Sans-Souci near Potsdam, which was built in 1754, won widespread fame.

By the middle of the eighteenth century the perfect setting for such architectural playthings had been developed by William Chambers in England. It was the Chinese garden. On the basis of the English type of garden, the casual lines of which were tailored to its particular landscape, Chambers fashioned garden compositions in which natural and man-made fantasies in the Chinese spirit were combined to create a type wholly novel to Europe (Fig. 29). A classic example of chinoiserie, the English-Chinese garden became the rage throughout Europe.

In residences and other formal buildings

planned more conservatively than those set in parks and gardens, the influence of China was less evident. Not that the doors of these structures were always closed to it. In such buildings chinoiserie, when used, was usually restricted to the decoration of certain rooms. No less an artist than Watteau painted a series of panels for a room in the Château de la Muette early in the eighteenth century. As we can now judge from the engravings made after Watteau's designs, these were arabesque panels in the early rococo style, to which fanciful chinoiserie figures were added. Other designers and decorators such as Bérain and Huquier worked in the same tradition of playful ornament (Fig. 30).

The artisans working in the several fields of the decorative arts were capable of supplying all the accessories needed to give any room a proper pseudo-Chinese character. Cabinet-makers, porcelain and pottery manufacturers, goldsmiths, silversmiths, tapestry weavers, silk weavers, makers of wallpaper, and the like, all at one time or another made use of the Chinese theme. Even wearing apparel reflected the passing mode. Gaily and charmingly, these varied arts pictured a chinoiserie world, and none more effectively than porcelain.

[4]

Nowhere was porcelain more enthusiastically taken up than in Germany, where various heads of state, following the example of the French court, vied with each other in their efforts to surround themselves with works in this material. "Porcelain rooms," containing both Chinese and European porcelains, were found in any number of palaces (Fig. 31), as at Ansbach, Charlottenburg, Schönbrunn, and Arnstadt, and in the Munich Residenz. In these curiously wayward examples of interior decoration, porcelains were not only used to embellish mantel-pieces but were placed on consoles as wall ornaments, and were even to be found as elements of the cornices.

The most ambitious project along these lines was never completed: the Japanese Palace at Dresden which Augustus the Strong, Elector of

Saxony and King of Poland, planned to decorate, room by room, exclusively with porcelain. Nevertheless, Augustus' great career as connoisseur and collector sums up all the contemporary European interest in the porcelain of China. Porcelain was his consuming passion, and he had the money and power to let his passion rule him. There has never, even in modern times, been a collector of Oriental wares who could vie with him. Augustus, the omnivorous collector, who once traded a regiment of dragoons for forty-eight vases, owned literally thousands of pieces.

FIGURE 31 *Porcelain room at Schloss Pommersfelden, near Bamberg, Germany*

FIGURE 32 *Chinoiserie in porcelain*

Chinese Emperor. Group from a table setting of porcelain made at the Höchst factory in Germany about 1765. Ex coll. R. Thornton Wilson. The Metropolitan Museum of Art

Yet in the story of porcelain Augustus has still a greater claim to fame. It was he who ordered the alchemist Johann Friedrich Böttger to turn his talents from a search for gold by the process of transmutation to a search for the secret of porcelain manufacture. Marvelously enough, Böttger succeeded. Thereafter Augustus could have his own porcelain—the very first hard-paste or true porcelain to be produced in the West—as well as his Chinese pieces. The factory at Meissen, near Dresden, where he established Böttger in 1710, was to prove to be the most brilliant in Europe, unequaled by the many factories that in the course of the century rose in imitation of it.

Other European factories, however, were distinguished in their own right and did their full share in meeting the increasing demand for the material. Earliest among Meissen's rivals was the Vienna factory established in 1719. Then there were factories at Höchst, Berlin, Fürstenburg, Nymphenburg, Frankenthal, and Ludwigsburg, all founded somewhat later, between 1750 and 1758. These all produced a true hard-paste porcelain. Elsewhere in Europe ceramists found difficulty in making this material. In France a substitute soft paste (*pâte tendre*) was made at Saint-Cloud, Chantilly, Mennecy, and Vincennes during the first half of the eighteenth century; it was not until 1769 that the Royal Manufactory at Sèvres succeeded in producing a hard-paste porcelain. In Italy a true porcelain was made in Venice as early as about 1720. At Capo-di-Monte, near Naples, soft-paste wares were made as early as 1743, and they were made at Buen Retiro, near Madrid, from 1759 on. In the several English factories, of which that at Chelsea was the earliest and one of the most distinguished—the Chelsea factory was active from about 1745 to 1784—a soft-paste porcelain was manufactured.

In porcelain, Europeans found themselves in possession of a medium which their master craftsmen fully exploited, thus adding new riches to the decorative arts of the West.

The output of the European factories was of two kinds: figures (Fig. 32) and tablewares. The former, which were used for table ornaments and for decoration throughout the house, are now the most sought after. The latter include most importantly the great dinner services and the smaller services for tea, coffee, and chocolate. These were the staple products upon which factory owners depended for their steady income.

The European dinner service varied in size according to the requirements of the buyer for whom it was made. A large service, such as one made at Meissen for Count Brühl, contained several hundred pieces. In content the services were much the same as those of our day, for during the great porcelain age of the eighteenth century the dinner service received the form it still possesses. It generally included platters, tureens, meat plates and soup plates, salad bowls, sauce boats, and mustard pots.

Services for tea, coffee, and chocolate formed a large part of European production. No less than eighty-four coffee services were described in the Meissen price list for the year 1760. And in the Chelsea catalogue for 1761, as well as in the catalogue of the liquidation sale of the Chelsea stock in 1785, many references are found to "compleat tea and coffee equipages." A typical equipage usually consisted of forty-one items: twelve teacups and saucers, six coffee cups and saucers, a teapot and stand, a slop "bason," a sugar "bason," and a cream ewer.

A few of the shapes occurring in European services, like the teapot and the teacup, are unquestionably of Chinese origin. Yet in the manner in which they were adapted to Western usage they differed from their Chinese prototypes. The shapes, which in China had been refined by the judgment of many generations, were on the whole simple and direct. The Chinese cup, for instance, was in the form of a small plain bowl and had no handle. When Europeans, less preoccupied with its formal beauty, began using hot beverages, they subtly altered the shape of the cup and added a handle. They furthermore placed a saucer under the cup.

A great many of the shapes are undoubtedly Western in origin. The meat plate, soup plate, and tureen, for example, are types commonly found in other European media such as silver, pewter, glass, or wood and sometimes actually originated in one of these other media. It is to be noted, also, that these basic forms, and the styles of decoration used by the Western porcelain painters, were much the same throughout all Europe. Not that forms and decorations ever remained static. They varied perceptibly from country to country and, in accordance with the evolution of style in eighteenth-century Europe, from decade to decade. These changes will give us reliable criteria for our classification of the China-Trade porcelains in the McCann collection. For, as we shall now discover, there was a highly significant relationship between the forms and decoration of Western porcelains and those of the China Trade.

CHINA-TRADE PORCELAIN

That European porcelains and those of the China Trade had many things in common is in no way surprising. Both answered to a demand in the West for utilitarian wares in the newly procurable material. Effective production for both began about the same time—early in the eighteenth century. Each seemed to promote the other, for the more widely porcelain became known in the West, the greater the clamor for both the European and the Chinese export varieties. The high points for the two wares as works of art came during the middle decades of the century. Thereafter a slow decline was to be observed in the quality of European porcelains and in the quantity of the China-Trade ware exported to the West. Their histories are closely bound together.

China-Trade porcelain, as was natural, varied in kind, in quality, and in other particulars. A great deal of it consisted of inexpensive household wares—either plain white or blue and white—which were manufactured in enormous quantities and shipped to the West wholesale. Finer wares, often of the *famille rose* type, that were specially decorated to Western order formed a lesser part of the export trade. As with other humble and fragile objects, little porcelain of the first type has survived. Many of the finer porcelains, however, have been preserved, and these wares for the most part make up the McCann collection and other private and public collections.

Nearly all the porcelains of the China Trade were made for use at the table, and most of the extant pieces are from services. Decorative vases and the like are infrequently found; figure groups of the type made at Meissen are hardly ever found. Dinner or hot-beverage services formed a large portion of the material sent from China to the West. The shapes, or forms, are generally European, and the painted decorations—at least those painted over the glaze at Canton—generally resemble those found on European pottery and porcelain. When forms of Chinese origin, such as the teacup, were used they were generally modified to conform to European taste. All these points may be noted in the Helena Woolworth McCann collection.

In the McCann collection there is evidence that a number of the models used by the Chinese were European porcelains and potteries sent to the Orient to be copied. But no evidence has been found that any of the European models were in other materials: silver, pewter, or glass. It is to be regretted that published documentary evidence which might disclose the nature of the models used for shape, and frequently for decoration, by the Chinese is almost completely lacking. One record bearing on the matter has, however, come to light. A document found in the archives of The Hague by I. G. A. N. de Vries states "that the Dutch East India Company had dispatched cases to China containing printed patterns of flowers and various ornamental motives . . . also models of French porcelain, notably the *pâtes tendres* of Sèvres," and that "the director [of the Dutch East India Company] especially requested that dragons and other chimerical animals should not be sent to Europe . . . but instead the small flowers in the taste of [the] Lowestoft ware [of England]." This undated notice, which gives support to our account of what must have happened, was published in 1936 by J. P. van Goidsenhoven in *La Céramique chinoise sous les Ts'ing*, a work in which the author drew upon a study by De Vries entitled *Porselein*.

It may be noted in passing that the printed patterns mentioned in the document at The Hague would appear to have been on the order of one executed in the chinoiserie style by Cornelis Pronck (1691–1759), an artist who entered the employ of the Dutch East India Company in 1734. A China-Trade plate decorated with this very composition (Fig. 33) shows that Pronck's design was actually used by Cantonese painters. Whether or not designs for ceramics like Pronck's were used to any considerable extent in the decorating of China-Trade porcelain cannot here be determined. None of the McCann porcelains seems to be connected with designs of this type.

The use of Western ceramic models in Canton increased in frequency during the course of the eighteenth century as the demand for China-Trade porcelain multiplied. With the sudden slackening of demand for the ware towards the end of the century there was a reversion to Oriental styles, especially in decoration.

The use of European models was, we believe, an inevitable development of the porcelain

FIGURE 33 *Plate of China-Trade porcelain and the Dutch design from which it was made*

Plate, J. P. van Goidsenhoven collection, Brussels; design, W. P. van Stockum & Zoon, The Hague

trade. Sending ceramic models to Canton—models which represented types of wares already familiar to Europeans—involved no particular problems. Models of this sort were comparatively inexpensive—much less costly, for example, than silverware—and could just as easily be sent to the Orient as Chinese porcelains could be sent to the West. The frequency with which models and copies can be identified suggests that many such models arrived in Canton. More important still, it reveals the export ware as representing an attractive collateral phase in the rise of porcelain in the West during that very period—the eighteenth century—when European porcelain reached its greatest heights.

[2]

A few Chinese porcelains which were made before 1715 bear European designs. None of this early type is in the McCann collection. These rarities were brought to the West by merchants visiting Canton before the establishment of the English factory there, and most of them date between 1699 and 1715, that is, after the arrival of the *Macclesfield*, the first English vessel ever to be welcomed by Cantonese authorities, and prior to the establishment of the factory. These pieces, frequently bearing armorial decoration, already show European and Chinese motives used in combination and in general may be said to be of the same type as the earliest porcelains in the McCann collection. For illustrations and fuller descriptions of such porcelains the interested reader should consult the works by Honey, Jenyns, and Tudor-Craig listed in the Bibliography.

Our study is concerned particularly with porcelains made between about 1715 and about 1820. They may be grouped according to style and chronology into three periods.

The first period, from about 1715 to about 1740, is one of experimentation in the making of an export ware that would satisfy the Western clients for whom it was intended. Chinese elements are considerably in evidence.

The more fully developed China-Trade style appears in the works of the second period, dating from about 1740 to about 1785, when European forms and decorations had become domesticated in Canton. This period represents the porcelain trade at its height, for it was then that the greater part of all the China-Trade ware was produced.

During the third and last period, from about 1785 to about 1820, a noticeable change took place: there was a gradual increase of Chinese elements in the painted decoration. This phenomenon became more marked as the final years of the century approached and as the great demand of the West abated. It was as though by its return to native Chinese designs this porcelain proclaimed its own decline as a distinguished international commodity. The end of this period—which, it may be noted, corresponds to the height of American trade to the Far Eastern market—truly marks the end of China-Trade porcelain as a significant art form.

[3]

The evidence available upon which a workable chronology for China-Trade porcelain may be based comprises, as we see it, four main categories: "dated" pieces; shape or form; armorial painted decoration; and non-armorial decoration, including both pictorial and repeat patterns.

Porcelains bearing dates are few. Generally such dates as there are exist as part of the porcelain decoration. Often their purpose is to commemorate a marriage, and for this reason they frequently appear under armorials or ciphers. If, as seems likely, such dated pieces were ordered on the occasion of a wedding, we may conclude, bearing in mind the span of time necessary for an order to reach Canton and for it to be executed, that the actual date of manufacture would normally be a year or two later than the "date" indicated on the porcelain.

A study of the shapes is generally helpful in dating porcelain. When a Western ceramic on which a China-Trade porcelain is directly based can be closely dated, we have evidence pointing toward the date of the Canton-painted version. For example, the Marieberg jardinière (see

FIGURE 34 *Three China-Trade teapots dating from 1750–1770*

Although their painted decorations differ in each instance, their shapes are all the same—indication that supplies of porcelain were stored in blank in the Canton workshops awaiting specific Western orders for their painted decoration. All are in the McCann collection. The Metropolitan Museum of Art.

page 158), which was copied almost exactly in China, was made between the years 1758 and 1766. Other Western ceramic types presumably used as models for China-Trade ware are illustrated in Figures 41 and 54.

In addition to this direct evidence, there is a less direct sort which relates to shapes that occur frequently in China-Trade porcelain. For example, on the evidence of "dates," armorial decorations, and designs inspired by European models, we find that the small teapot with round bowl, plain handle, straight spout, and domed top is common in the middle decades of the century. It does not seem to have been in use after about 1775. Of Oriental origin, the form had been quickly adopted by Europe, and in the China Trade it may be considered to be quite as European as Chinese. It is the simplest and most perfect of all teapot forms. Three China-Trade examples are illustrated in Figure 34. Their designs, which differ from one another, will be noted in the text accompanying Plates 41, 57, and 64. Their shapes are identical. The

occurrence of different designs on identical shapes would seem to confirm the suggestion set forth on page 36 that Cantonese workshops kept in storage ample supplies of unpainted porcelains from Chingtechen, awaiting orders for their decoration that might come from any of the European factories at Canton.

The same kinds of evidence mentioned above indicate that the cylinder-shaped teapot which also occurs often in China-Trade ware was not made before about 1780. An early example is illustrated in Plate 45. Specialists have generally supposed that the form of this type of pot was based on that of English silver teapots sent to Canton as models for the export wares. True enough, the shape is European, but its origin would seem to be found not in silver but in English ceramic wares, for example, in the Worcester teapot illustrated on page 124, which is dated between 1765 and 1770. This English example has the same general shape as the Chinese versions. It has, besides, what English silver teapots never have, an interlaced handle. Typical of much English ceramic work, especially that of Leeds, this form of handle is exactly the same as that found almost without exception on all the cylinder-shaped teapots of the China Trade.

Armorial decoration, our next category of evidence, is a most important one since armorial bearings figure so frequently on China-Trade porcelains. As we shall see when we come to

55

discuss particular pieces, we sometimes know the histories of the individuals for whom armorially decorated porcelains were made. Such information obviously throws light on the porcelains made for them. Armorial decorations on chinaware are also of value in determining an approximate dating even when the bearings are not identified. For there was a development in the European styles of representing armorial bearings, one that is perhaps most evident from a study of armorial bookplates. These heraldic fashions are often described by the terms "baroque," "rococo" or "chippendale," and "neo-classic," none of them exact terms, but all in common usage. The baroque armorial is florid, balanced, and often large in scale; the rococo, lighter and asymmetrical; and the neo-classic, balanced and frequently extremely simple. Characteristic examples of each style are shown in Figure 35. Since the styles are at least approximately datable, the presence of arms on China-Trade wares is usually informative.

Although it has been frequently stated that armorial bookplates served as models for the Cantonese, no examples of chinaware with decorations based on bookplate models are

known to us. Actually there seems to be far more variation in bookplate armorial ornament than in that found on chinaware. This, together with the fact that certain armorial enframements seem to have been repeated on various chinaware services (see page 92), suggests that the East India Company traders may well have furnished the Cantonese painters with stock designs for armorial enframements which the latter became adept at using and which they could apply to a variety of services.

Decoration other than armorial gives us another basis for dating the China-Trade porcelains that were decorated to order. It exists in several varieties. There are the pictorial decorations, both in black-and-white wares and those in colors, based on European prints and drawings; the decorative patterns based on European ceramic models; the pictorial or ornament designs of purely Chinese origin; and the designs developed in Chingtechen and Canton specially for the export trade.

When the pictorial decoration of a China-Trade porcelain can be identified with a datable source—perhaps a dated European print—we may be sure that the porcelain was painted after the original was made.

A number of European prints and drawings seem to have been used as models by Cantonese designers. These subjects were generally secular and reflected the diversity of European fashions current in art when they were made. Many are

FIGURE 35 *Armorial styles of the XVIII century represented in English bookplates*

These are typical examples of the application of the baroque, rococo, and neo-classic styles to heraldry.

56

of classical inspiration—during the eighteenth century the gods of Olympus were familiar figures in the workshops of Canton. A few porcelains, appropriately enough for such a sea-borne material, were decorated with marine subjects. There were also porcelains with decorations of a religious nature.

The religious porcelains with decorations generally painted in black on white are of especial interest. They are known as "Jesuit" china. As far as can be determined, however, there is no evidence of any connection between the so-called Jesuit china and the works of the Jesuits in China. The facts as we have them tell another story.

The genesis of the term Jesuit china is often connected with the following passage from Father d'Entrecolles's letter of 1712 describing Chingtechen:

From the debris at a large emporium [in the town] they brought me a little plate which I treasure more than the finest porcelain made during the last thousand years. In the center of the plate is painted a crucifix between the Virgin and St. John, and I am told that this kind of porcelain was shipped sometimes to Japan, but that this commerce came to an end sixteen or seventeen years ago.

Father d'Entrecolles, apparently the first Jesuit to know Chingtechen, was well versed in the history of Chinese porcelain. Yet he was surprised to come across the Crucifixion plate. He would have been more surprised if he had known that the plate could very well have been made not for any adherent of his faith but for the Protestant Dutch who at that time were trading with Japan and who seem to have been able to place orders with Chinese merchants. Furthermore, the typical extant examples of Jesuit china were painted in Canton nearly half a century later than Father d'Entrecolles's report and seem to have been based, if indirectly, on European ceramic models such as the Delft plate of the Crucifixion made between 1720 and 1730 (see page 134). In dating Jesuit wares—for

FIGURE 36 *Some border designs of European derivation seen in China-Trade porcelains*

ABOVE: "Lacework" border after a mid-XVIII-century Meissen style. See Plate 55. CENTER: Interweaving border after a late XVIII-century English ceramic style. See Plates 94, 95. BELOW: Grape border after Western ceramic models. See Plate 99.

which we now suggest as a more correct designation the term black-and-white wares—we must, therefore, rely on considerations of style rather than on the evidence of Father d'Entrecolles's letter.

Still another basis for dating China-Trade porcelain is to be found in the formal decorations—especially those for the embellishment of borders—which are mainly inspired by the ornament of Western ceramics (Fig. 36). The approximate date of any given piece of Western ceramic ware is usually known. Therefore, the porcelain decorations used at Meissen, Worcester, and other ceramic centers of the West indicate the date of reflections of them produced in the Cantonese workshops.

Other elements are derived from Chinese sources—particularly the decoration of Chinese porcelains. These prove more troublesome to deal with than those based on Western designs.

FIGURE 37 *The spear-head border and two Chinese border motives suggested as origins for it*

LEFT: Border on the rim of a China-Trade mug, dated 1758, in the McCann collection (shown also in Plate 33). CENTER: Motive on a porcelain ewer of the Yung Chêng period (1723–1735). Chinese National collection. RIGHT: Motive on a porcelain vase of the Ch'ien Lung period (1736–1795). Musée Guimet, Paris

The fact is that the dating of Chinese porcelains made for home consumption is hardly ever precise. Chinese porcelains bearing decoration which might throw light on the origins of wares made for the Western market are described by specialists in the field merely as "of the Ch'ien Lung period." And this, it may be noted, is a designation covering the entire six decades of that emperor's rule (1736–1795); it is also the period of nearly all the porcelains found in the McCann collection.

Finally, there are the designs developed in China especially for the export trade. These were neither purely European nor purely Chinese. They were true hybrids. A few of the more characteristic types may here be pointed out, since they are important for the dating of the export ware and will be met with frequently during the course of our study of the McCann collection.

One of the most commonly used of these motives is the so-called spear-head border. Seemingly it was created in Canton for the China Trade as a simplification of the lambrequin border found on earlier Chinese porcelains of the eighteenth century (Fig. 37). Whatever its origin, it immediately became popular with Europeans, for its fleur-de-lis-like shape appears to have evoked, even though by chance, vague memories of Western decorative forms such as those used by Herold in the painting of Meissen

porcelain. This spear-head border was usually painted in gold and outlined in red. It was long in vogue and is found on a number of pieces which because of "dates," armorial bearings, or decorations in the European manner can be placed in the 1740s, the 1750s, and the 1760s. Thereafter, except in debased form, it soon disappeared from the ornament vocabulary of the Cantonese porcelain painters. The motive stands, then, as a reliable sign of mid-eighteenth-century workmanship.

Another border pattern frequently met with is the one known for some obscure reason as "Fitzhugh" (Plate 104). It suggests a Chinese landscape with rocks, flowers, and butterflies. This pattern, which is always painted under the glaze, is actually the work of the Chingtechen

FIGURE 38 *Some Cantonese border designs on China-Trade porcelains of the 1780s and 1790s*

TOP: Narrow line of dart-like elements, a motive used before 1785. See Plate 45. SECOND: Dotted fillings within interlaced compartments, a motive indicating late XVIII-century workmanship. See Plates 80, 82; also Plates 85, above, and 90. THIRD: Blue band sown with gold stars, a motive popular with Americans in the 1790s. See Plate 85, below. FOURTH: Chinese meander pattern. See Plate 96.

porcelain painters; it is more pronouncedly Chinese in character than the typical Canton-decorated porcelains, perhaps because it was developed so far from Canton, where the Western traders were located. It seems to have been used as early as the 1770s, and it continued in ever more conventionalized form well into the nineteenth century. It was the basis of the willow pattern which was later developed by English potters.

In the 1780s and 1790s a variety of narrow bandings came into fashion, all of which were produced for the China Trade at Canton (Fig. 38). Among these perhaps the most common is the one composed of tiny interlaced compartments containing dotted fillings. Another popular border of this period is a narrow band decorated with tiny stars. These types and variants of them will be met with in our study of the McCann collection.

Such are the types of evidence upon which may be based a chronology for the wares exported to the West. It should be here noted, however, that, since American entry into Far Eastern trade came towards the end of the significant European trade in porcelain, some of this evidence does not apply directly to the wares made for the American market.

Two of the types of evidence apply equally to European and American wares: that of "dated" pieces and that of shape. As in the pieces made for Europe, some of the porcelains destined for America bear dates. And the evidence of shape holds for both American and European pieces, for there was almost no ceramic ware of American manufacture that might serve as models for the Chinese potters.

China-Trade porcelain made for America varies most significantly from that made for Europe in respect to painted decoration, although there were often close resemblances as well as striking variations. Among the pictorial decorations marine subjects held a high place in the affections of American buyers, as is attested by the many porcelains so decorated that still exist. Others commemorate important events in American history, as, for example, the death of Washington. In those strongly republican days ciphers offered a convenient substitute for family armorials, and often appeared on porcelains imported from China. Armorial decoration, when used, generally appeared in a patriotic context, and the Great Seal of the United States and the arms of individual states were widely employed. Masonic emblems and the badge of the Order of the Cincinnati were frequently chosen by members of those organizations. Some of the characteristically American emblems were often used in conjunction with underglaze decoration such as the Fitzhugh border—a type of decoration as popular in America as in Europe.

[4]

As we know by now, there were two chief types of porcelain: the more common wares which were either left undecorated or were decorated at Chingtechen under the glaze, chiefly in blue; and the more costly wares which were decorated over the glaze in Canton.

The few pieces of the former variety in the McCann collection were for the most part made towards the end of the porcelain trade, within the 1785–1820 period. These underglaze porcelains are sometimes decorated with Fitzhugh borders. Chinese landscapes and Chinese symbolic motives were also used. In addition to underglaze blue, red-orange and green were the colors most frequently used, although none of these ever appear together on the same piece. Sometimes enameled armorial decorations were added at Canton.

Such porcelains were often known as Nanking, or Nankeen, ware (see page 8), after the river port on the Yangtze. As already indicated, it seems likely that this type of ware was commonly shipped in wholesale lots from Chingtechen, by Nanking, to Canton—a route that lay entirely by water. The opening of other Chinese ports to Western traders after the Opium War of the 1840s made it no longer necessary to send such porcelain to Canton (for its painted decoration had been completed at Chingtechen), and some very late examples of the ware may have been dispatched directly from Nanking to the West. No porcelains were actually made in Nanking.

Even the commonest of these underglaze, or Nanking, porcelains reveal an easy ability in painting which betokens full mastery of the porcelain painter's craft and attests the continuing strength of the tradition that obtained in Chingtechen. Compared to these works, the carefully delineated painted porcelains emanating from the Cantonese workshops seem on occasion crabbed and artificial.

As for the porcelains painted in Canton, many of these were in the *famille rose* style, though there were, of course, exceptions, such as those painted in black in the manner of Western engravings. Because of the importance of this *famille rose* style for the full understanding of China-Trade ware, we describe it in some detail. Its history, like that of the export porcelain itself, is a curious one that makes it a singularly appropriate style for the ware's decoration.

The term *famille rose* designates the most popular style of porcelain painting in eighteenth-century China and includes all porcelains in which one of the enamel pigments is of an opaque rose-pink color. Strangely enough, the rose color was first used not as might be expected in China but in Europe. It is derived from a salt of gold which in the West was called Purple of Cassius, having received its name from Andreas Cassius of Leyden, a physician and chemist, who in the middle of the seventeenth century had been the first to produce the hue. According to W. C. Honey, in *The Ceramic Art of China*, the earliest use of this color in pottery probably occurred among such Nuremberg enamelers as Wolf Rössler about 1680.

Honey notes that some Chinese also attribute the origins of the rose color to the West. "The rose-pink and the other opaque colours associated with it were known as *yang ts'ai* ('foreign colours'), or as *juan ts'ai* ('soft colours'), to the Chinese, who have obscurely referred to Western enamelling ('*fa lang*'), either *cloisonné* or painted in the Canton manner, as the source

from which they were derived." One Chinese source suggests how the color actually may have come to China. In the most authoritative Chinese work on porcelain written in the eighteenth century, the *Ching-tê-chên T'ao Lu*, enamels of this variety are said to have been first made at *Ku-li* (the Chinese name for the Indian port of Calicut), indicating that they may have been carried by traders from Europe to China by way of India. This seems to be a reasonable assumption.

There were many gradations in the hues derived from Purple of Cassius, and all of these are to be found in examples of China-Trade ware. These variations were due entirely to the firing. The process of establishing the particular tone was quite simple. Once the enamel painters had done their work, the wares were placed in an oven, or muffle stove, small in relation to the great furnaces of Chingtechen. The heat was then raised until the desired shade of pink was attained. As the heat began to affect the enamel, a red-brown color appeared; this, as greater heat was applied, gave place to rose and finally to violet. According to Williamson, the best rose color was obtained at about 800° centigrade. This temperature may be compared with the 1500° of heat needed for the manufacture of the porcelain itself in the furnaces of Chingtechen.

It seems likely that the Cantonese developed their technique of enameling porcelains as an adaptation of the technique of painting in enamel on copper. This last was a well-established craft in Canton, and it also had European origins, being based on the art that had its inception in centers such as Limoges in France. Knowledge of this technique seems to have been brought to Canton no earlier than the seventeenth century.

In the eighteenth century a relationship of the closest sort evidently existed in the Canton factories between enameling on copper and porcelain painting. In the McCann collection there is to be found among the enameled porcelains in the great service made for the Portuguese family of Saldanha de Albuquerque a considerable number of dishes and covers of enameled copper. Both the porcelain and the copper vessels were surely painted by the artisans of a single shop, the style and manner of painting being the same in each case.

That both the rose color and the enamel-based method of applying that color were first developed in the West stands as a vivid commentary on the involved nature of the intercommunication of styles and techniques by means of which the arts of far distant regions continually enrich one another.

THE McCANN COLLECTION

THE HELENA WOOLWORTH McCANN COLLECTION OF CHINA-TRADE PORCELAIN

Only a few collectors have been so ardent or so successful as Helena Woolworth McCann was in her chosen field, China-Trade porcelain. Discerningly she selected pieces of the most splendid and colorful design. Her collection is a delight to the eye, and consists of examples which in the days of the China Trade had been produced with the greatest care for the most knowing of Western buyers. It contains very few of the blue-and-white porcelains which were generally dispatched in vast quantities to the West. Indeed, one can safely say that no collection represents with more distinction the China-Trade ware at the peak of its popularity.

As a collector Mrs. McCann intuitively realized the advantage that lay in the possession of complete dinner and tea services. Individually, the pieces forming such services have their own beauty. Collectively, they often add up to something quite dazzling. Museums, with their problems of space limitation and of guardianship, would hardly ever be able to exhibit complete services. But Mrs. McCann was able to do so. The many services she treasured were regularly used for her table at Sunken Orchard, her Long Island residence (Fig. 39). The splendid effect achieved by such a presentation is to be imagined.

Some two dozen dinner services (more or less complete) account for 3,000 of the approximately 4,000 pieces in the collection. About a dozen tea services (again more or less complete) account for another 400. The remaining 600 include pieces from many services as well as single objects made for a variety of useful purposes—an inkstand, a watch stand, vases, and the like.

The typical collector is apt to specialize in wares destined for one region: the Continent, England, or America. Mrs. McCann collected without regard to the market for which a piece was made, but since most export ware was made to European order the material she gathered together consists largely of porcelains made for the Continent or England. There is also a representative group made for America, and a handful made for trade to India, then under British rule. Although the examples of the ware made for America are few in comparison to those made for Europe, they seem to represent American-market porcelain in its correct relation to the porcelain trade as a whole. Of the porcelains made for Europe, the majority were directed to the English market, and this is hardly surprising in view of the long dominance of the English East India Company in Canton. A notable group of McCann porcelains was made for the Portuguese. Other "European" pieces represent a variety of Continental markets, particularly Scandinavia, Germany, and Holland. Together these 4,000 pieces reflect the variety and the extent of the trade in Chinese porcelain throughout the Western world in the eighteenth and the early nineteenth century.

The collection is not merely described as a whole in general terms; it is recorded and interpreted by presenting in plates and in commentary a number of significant porcelains in what seems to be their chronological sequence. Various other services are treated in an Appendix.

In order to set down the chronological sequence of the McCann porcelains in the clearest form possible, we divide the material into three main groups. The first group dates from about 1715—the moment of the establishment of the English East India Company at Canton—to about 1740. The second extends from about 1740 to about 1785. The third, from about 1785 to about 1820. It may be observed that the porcelains made for America and for British India both fall within the limits of the third group and are treated separately, following the material made for the European market.

FIGURE 39 *Woodwork of the Louis XV period installed in the Museum of Fine Arts, Boston, as a setting for China-Trade porcelains from the McCann collection*

The paneling, given by the Winfield Foundation, was formerly in the Porcelain Room at Sunken Orchard, Mrs. McCann's Long Island residence.

PLATE I

Platter with the arms of Townshend impaling Harrison. English market

ABOUT 1725

PLATE 2

Tureen with the arms of Newton (Alleyne in pretense). English market

1740–1750

PLATE 3

Plate with unidentified arms. Continental market

1760–1770

PLATE 4

Teapot with the Hayes arms. English market

1760–1770

PLATE 5

Plate with the Snoeck arms. Dutch market

1760–1770

PLATE 6   *Tureen and platter with the arms of Saldanha de Albuquerque surmounted by the insignia of a bishop. Portuguese market*
1760–1770

PLATE 7 *Tureen and sauce boat bearing the Gordon arms. English market*
1770–1785

PLATE 8

Plate with a representation of the Resurrection. Continental market?

1750–1770

PLATE 9

Dish with a copy of The Embroideress. Dutch market?

1750–1770

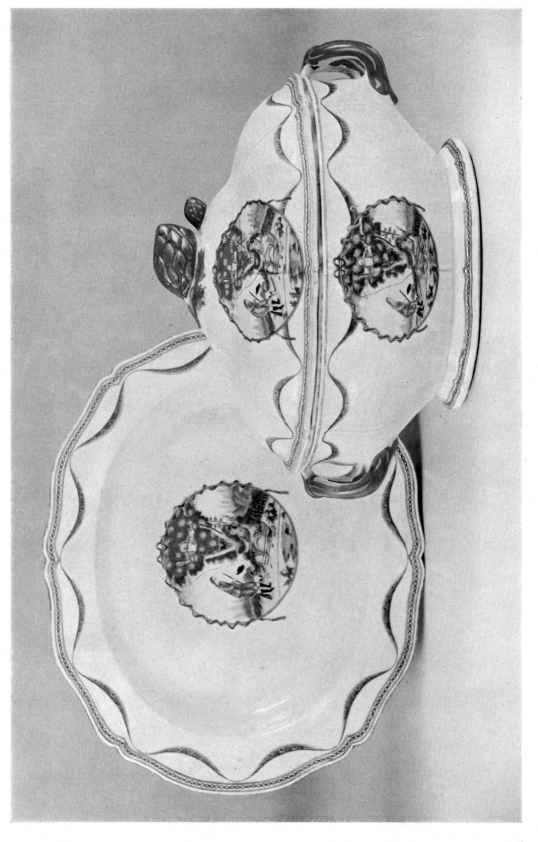

PLATE 10   *Tureen and platter with a scene showing a hunter and a lady. Continental market*
1750–1770

PLATE II

*Jardinière after a pottery
model produced at the
Marieberg factory. Swedish
market*

1760–1770

PLATE 12   *Punch bowl showing peasant boys astride water buffalo. European market*
1750–1775

PLATE 13 *Punch bowl showing peasant boys working on a haystack. English or Continental market*
1785–1800

PLATE 14   *Dish and creamer bearing the Hammond arms. English market*
1785–1800

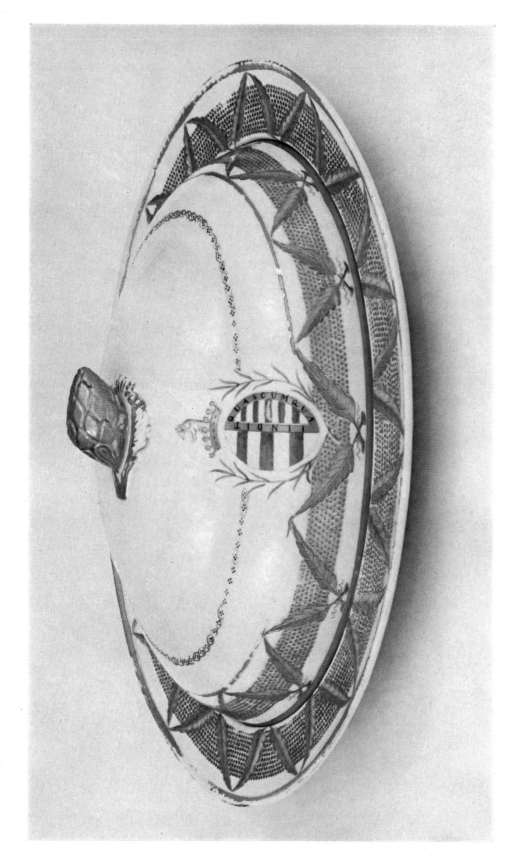

PLATE 15   *Covered dish with the arms of Silveira impaling Tavora. Portuguese market*
1785–1800

THE HELENA WOOLWORTH McCANN COLLECTION

PLATE 16 *Tureen with Fitzhugh border decoration, the arms of the United States, and an unidentified monogram.*

American market

EARLY XIX CENTURY

PORCELAINS OF
1715-1740

China-Trade porcelains of this period frequently possess a boldness of design that is lacking among the more standardized wares of the later decades of the century. Although a number of their forms, or shapes, are already basically Western and seem to follow Western ceramic models, their painted decorations usually have strong Oriental overtones. This exotic element may have been one of the attractions of the ware, for through imported Ming and K'ang-hsi porcelains Westerners had become accustomed to the Oriental idiom. Furthermore, at a time when porcelain was only beginning to be manufactured in Europe the domestic ceramic wares afforded little that could vie in quality with Chinese painted decorations. These factors, together with the general enthusiasm for chinoiserie, seem to account for the prevalence of Oriental decorations on European ceramics of the first half of the eighteenth century, a phenomenon faithfully reflected in the painted decorations of the early China-Trade porcelains.

PORCELAINS WITH
ARMORIAL DECORATIONS
1715–1740

Perhaps the most ancient of all the porcelains in the McCann collection are a ewer and basin (Plate 17) made as part of a service for one of the notable personalities of eighteenth-century England. James Brydges, first Duke of Chandos, was a splendid figure. Everyone of his generation knew of the great house at Canons, near Edgeware, where Alexander Pope and George Frederick Handel were numbered among the many distinguished guests. There were a hundred servants at Canons, and a choir, for which Handel supplied no less than twenty anthems, was daily in attendance to entertain at dinner.

It was for this London town house that the ewer and basin were made. They bear the arms of Brydges and Willoughby and must therefore have been made some time between 1713, when the Duke was married to Cassandra Willoughby, and 1744, when he died. Their decoration, save for the heraldic detail, which is very much in the "baroque" manner, is quite Chinese. The similarity of style of the Chandos pieces to a plate in the Tudor-Craig collection made for the Right Honorable James Craggs, who became Principal Secretary of State for George I in 1710 and who died in 1721, suggests that the ewer and basin may also have been made prior to 1721. It is interesting to note that the form of the ewer, with a mask under its spout, is similar to that frequently found not only in European metalwares but in European ceramics of the time.

A hexagonal plate (Plate 1) with the arms of Townshend impaling Harrison is of about the same period as the ewer and basin. The family coat of Harrison was added to the Townshend shield after the marriage of Baron Townshend de Lynn Regis and Audrey Harrison of Balls Park in 1723, so the plate was made after that date. But not long after, for it is close in style to an octagonal plate bearing the arms of Sir John Lambert, a Director of the South Sea Company, who died in February 1723. It is likely that the service from which the Townshend plate comes was made on the occasion of the Baron's wedding. Its painted decoration of Chinese trees within the border area is carried out in underglaze blue and was surely applied at Chingtechen before the porcelain was shipped to Canton. The baroque arms painted in full tincture over the glaze were, of course, added in some Cantonese workshop. It may be noted that the emblazonment is large in relation to the size of the plate. This is also true of the pieces made for the Duke of Chandos, although in our illustration (Plate 17) only the crest is fully visible. The rendering of arms so large in proportion to the porcelain surface is generally an indication of early date in China-Trade wares.

Another example of the early type of armorial china is the plate bearing the Harries arms (Plate 18). Unfortunately, it is not possible to identify the particular member of the family to whom these arms belonged. Since the bearings alone offer little help in the matter of dating, we must be guided by considerations of style in determining the age of this plate. We note, for example, the shield's baroque shape, its abundant mantling, and its generous scale in relation to the surrounding area—all indications of an early date.

PLATE 17

Ewer and basin with the arms of James Brydges, first Duke of Chandos. English market

1715–1725

PLATE 18

Plate with the arms of Harries. English market

ABOUT 1740

PORCELAINS WITH
NON-ARMORIAL DECORATIONS
1725–1740

Perhaps the rarest of all the McCann porcelains are the cup and saucer decorated with scenes showing the interior of a chinaware shop in Canton (Frontispiece). The impression these scenes give us of the city's commercial life was noted on page 96. Considered purely as porcelain, these pieces are of the finest eggshell variety; and their painting is precise. They correspond more closely than do most China-Trade wares to porcelains made by the Chinese for their own use. From the point of view of style they may be related to porcelains made during the reign of the Emperor Yung Chêng (1723–1735). The gilt foliate patterning of the borders, broken at intervals by tiny cartouches enclosing Chinese scenes, is much like the broad blue border on the Townshend plate (Plate 1), which may have been made about 1725.

A shaving bowl (Plate 19) and a tureen (Plate 20) and platter provide further examples of the work of this period. Their decorations show the continuance of designs that are mainly Oriental in character. As their colors are principally variations of rose, these porcelains are related to the *famille rose* wares then being produced in great quantities for the Chinese home market.

PLATE 20

Tureen with Oriental floral decoration. European market 1725–1740

PORCELAINS OF
1740-1785

The years from about 1740 to about 1785 were the golden period of the trade in Chinese porcelain. The making of china for export to the West was now an established business involving thousands of workers and complicated dealings with representatives of many Western nations.

The trade in porcelains from about 1715 to about 1740 was largely monopolized by the English, who were the first to establish a factory for trade in Canton. By 1740, however, the various European East India Companies—the Dutch, the French, the Swedish, the Danish, and others—had settled in their own commodious factories lined up in file along the Canton riverbank and were taking back rich cargoes of China-Trade porcelain to their home ports. Theirs was a prosperous, expanding market.

The porcelains of this period have a different character from those of the preceding group in that the designs are more completely Europeanized, a change possibly to be explained by the revival of the European ceramics industry brought about by Böttger's discovery of the secret of hard-paste porcelain. By 1750 the mak-ing of porcelain in the West, as we have already seen (page 50), was no longer tentative and experimental. In the factories at Meissen and elsewhere in Europe new standards for the form and decoration of porcelain had been set—standards that have remained relatively unchanged down to our own times. Europe now had its own porcelain and its own manner of decorating the material and found them good—so good, in fact, that a reasonable facsimile of Western wares was demanded in the porcelains ordered from Canton.

In porcelains of this group we find that the forms more and more approximate those of Europe—outright copies can sometimes be identified—and that the decorations, too, have become as European as the untutored but willing Cantonese painters could make them. Armorial porcelains continued in demand, but an innovation which gives this group its greatest interest was the development of wares with pictorial decorations. These were copied from prints, from drawings, or directly from European porcelains sent to China to serve as models. Among the pictorial pieces was the so-called Jesuit china bearing religious subjects. Various scenes of purely secular interest were also represented and, appropriately enough for such a sea-borne material, a number of porcelains were decorated with marine subjects.

PORCELAINS WITH
ARMORIAL DECORATIONS
1740–1785

The earliest pieces in this group are of a transitional type, for, although they may have been made in the 1740s, they continue to show strongly Chinese designs typical of the period from 1715 to 1740.

Outstanding among these is the first of the great dinner services that form so conspicuous a part of the McCann collection: that made for a member of the Newton family. Not the least extraordinary thing about the Newton service (Plates 2 and 21) is the composition of the arms themselves. The bearings of Newton (Alleyne in pretense) are macabre—crossed human bones upon a large black shield form the background for the smaller central shield. The gilded sprays which also adorn the service are Chinese in character.

There are altogether 81 pieces in this service, which in its entirety may have comprised well over 200. There are 55 dinner plates, 12 soup plates, 9 large round dishes or platters, 1 deep dish, 2 tureens with covers, and 2 mugs. It is to be noted that, although the decoration is Chinese, the forms are, on the whole, based on ceramic prototypes of the West. The Newton type of tureen, for example, seemingly finds its model in the productions of the German potters.

Related in style to the Newton service are a plate (Plate 22) and a wine cooler (Plate 23), both with unidentified arms. Their partially gilded floral sprays are typical of the style of the porcelain painters of Canton. The wine cooler is distinctly European in form.

A number of porcelains made early in the period show a style that is quite as European as it is Oriental. The first of these is a platter bearing the Farington arms (Plate 24). Its noncommittal border of green and gold is kept to a minimum; the arms, carefully drawn and colored, are the beginning and end of decorative interest. Simply on the evidence of the style of its armorial decoration the Farington platter seems to have been made just before the middle of the eighteenth century. An armorial platter with almost identical framing, made for Ralph Bigland, Garter King of Arms, is dated by Tudor-Craig "circa 1740."

One of the most interesting sets in the McCann collection is the tea service with the arms of Seymour (Plates 25 and 26). It presently consists of more than 50 pieces. The service was presumably made for Algernon Seymour, seventh Duke of Somerset, who inherited his title in 1748 and died only two years later. The possibility that the service was ordered about the time of the Duke's accession accords with the stylistic evidence, for various related pieces illustrated in Tudor-Craig's *Armorial Porcelain* are dated between 1745 and 1750. The Duchy of Somerset, incidentally, was created in the sixteenth century by Henry VIII for the eldest brother of Jane Seymour, at a time when she was queen. Beneath the arms, which are supported by a blue bull and a white unicorn wearing gold crowns for collars, is the Seymour motto: FOY POUR DEVOIR.

Similar in period to the Seymour equipage is the magnificent table service with the arms of the Dukes of Anhalt, of which nearly 100 pieces are to be found in the McCann collection (Plates 27 and 28). Capped by its ducal crown, and proudly set against a mantling of ermine, this Germanic design is unsurpassed for sheer heraldic splendor by any of the other McCann porcelains. As with the Farington platter, it is the arms, faithfully copied, which furnish the design interest. In the tureen (Plate 27) the arms cascade boldly over the cover and down the vessel's side. It seems likely that the service was made for Leopold II, who became Duke in 1747 and died in 1751. The Duke was a general in the army of Frederick the Great of Prussia, and his father, Leopold I, is credited with the creation of Frederick's incomparable infantry.

The McCann collection richly represents armorial porcelain of the 1750s. Take, for example, the tureen and monteith (Plates 29 and 30), which may have been ordered for some Spanish noble family. The central shield is encircled by the collar of the Order of the Knights of Malta, and the heraldic detail also seems to be Spanish; nevertheless, the arms remain unidentified. Spanish or not, in the manner of the representation of the arms the porcelains are closely related to the Anhalt pieces, which we have placed about 1750. Other elements in their decoration, however—both the puce-colored floral swags and the narrow chain border in gold—are more characteristic of Cantonese work of the 1750s. The floral swags of classical inspiration are obviously of European origin, and Tudor-Craig, presumably on the evidence of heraldic designs, places a number of services in which ornament of this type occurs in the 1750s. The chain border seems to be a convention developed by Cantonese porcelain painters towards the middle of the eighteenth century.

Also of the 1750s are the garniture of five vases of Oriental shape (Plate 32) and a tea service represented by 30 pieces in the McCann collection (a selection is illustrated in Plate 31). These fine examples of Chinese craftsmanship all show the same unidentified arms with an antelope head as crest. Each of the vases shows two car-touches, one with the arms, the other, painted in *famille rose* colors, with a picture of a bird in a landscape. The conventionalized floral pattern of the ground is worked in relief, white on white, a method not uncommon in Chinese porcelain during the period of Ch'ien Lung (1736–1795). These China-Trade pieces seem to be related in style to certain pieces made for the Scandinavian market, but that is only a guess. In the tea service the spear-head border, a motive found in the 1740s, the 1750s, and the 1760s, forms an essential part of the design.

Among the armorial wares in the McCann collection are five pieces which may be dated close to 1760. The first, a mug (Plate 33), is of unusual interest in that under its bold cipher is inscribed the date 1758, which may relate to the marriage of the original owners. The spear-head border is in evidence upon its rim.

Armorial style indicates that two jugs (Plate 34) also are of a similar date. The one at the right of the illustration may actually have been ordered in 1760 or shortly thereafter, for the arms it bears are those of Mawbey impaling Pratt. It is recorded that Sir Joseph Mawbey, first Baronet of Botleys, married Elizabeth Pratt in 1760. It may be noted that the rococo handle of the jug at the left is of a type frequently found on English ceramics of the period.

A platter bearing the arms of Holburn (Plate 36) and three small vignettes—a landscape in the center and two water-front scenes in the border—may on the basis of the form of the armorial insignia also be assigned to about 1760. The very same scenes occur on a plate with another coat of arms, in this instance unidentified (Plate 35). Evidently the decoration of the two plates was copied from a model kept in readiness for just such use in one of the Cantonese workshops where porcelain was painted.

PLATE 21

Mug with the arms of Newton (Alleyne in pretense). English market
1740–1750

PLATE 22

Plate with unidentified arms. Continental market?

1740–1750

PLATE 24

Platter with the Farington arms. English market

PLATE 25

Cup and saucer with the arms of Algernon Seymour, seventh Duke of Somerset. English market

ABOUT 1750

PLATE 26

Teapot and slop bowl with the arms of Algernon Seymour, seventh Duke of Somerset. English market

ABOUT 1750

PLATE 27

Tureen and platter with the arms of the Dukes of Anhalt. German market

ABOUT 1750

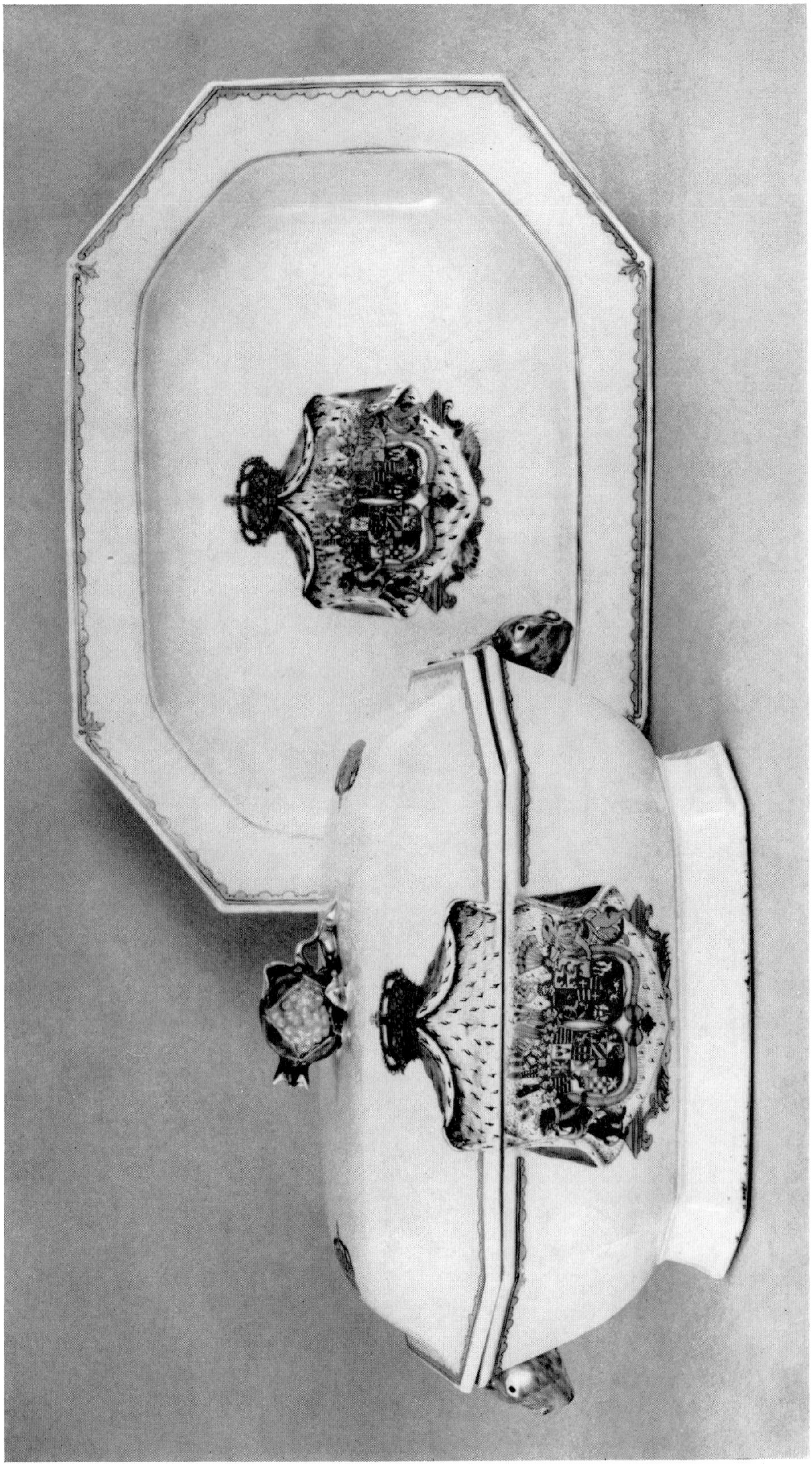

PLATE 28

Platter and two dishes with the arms of the Dukes of Anhalt. German market

ABOUT 1750

PLATE 29

Tureen with unidentified arms encircled by the collar of the Knights of Malta. Spanish market?
1750–1760

PLATE 30

Monteith with unidentified arms encircled by the collar of the Knights of Malta. Spanish market?

1750–1760

PLATE 31

Selected pieces from a tea service bearing unidentified arms. Scandinavian market?
1750–1760

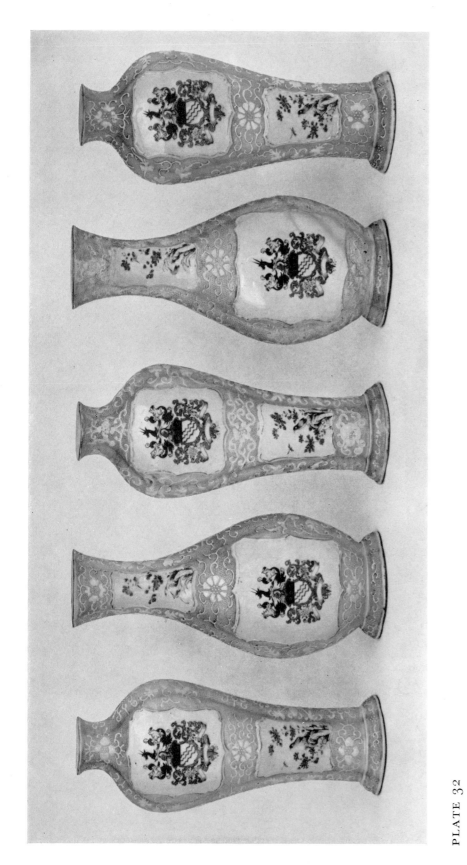

PLATE 32

Garniture of vases with unidentified arms. Scandinavian market?
1750–1760

PLATE 33
Mug with unidentified crest and cipher, and the date 1758. Continental market

PLATE 34

Left: *Jug with unidentified arms. English market*

Right: *Jug with the arms of Mawbey impaling Pratt. English market*

ABOUT 1760

PLATE 35

Plate with unidentified arms.

English market

ABOUT 1760

PLATE 36

*Platter with the
Holburn arms.
English market*
ABOUT 1760

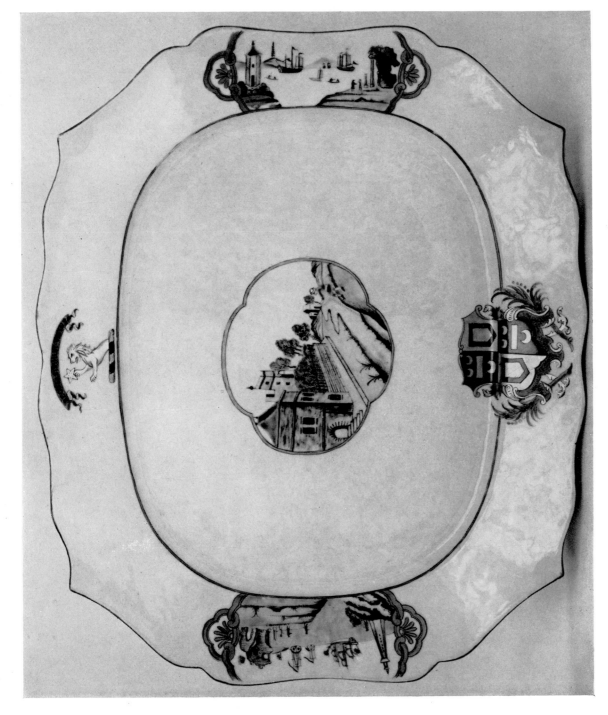

PORCELAINS WITH
ARMORIAL DECORATIONS
1760–1770

A new armorial style is evident in the McCann porcelains of the 1760s. It is the style called "rococo" (or "Chippendale" or "middle Georgian"), and characterized by the fact that the shield or its surrounding ornament is rendered asymmetrically.

A remarkable dinner service with arms that are just slightly rococo was made for a member of the Saldanha family (Plates 6, 37, and 38), perhaps as early as 1760. The name SALDANHA DE ALBUQUERQUE figures in the design, and it is said that the set was presented by an Indian maharajah to a member of that family who was active in Indo-Portuguese affairs. That this personage was an ecclesiastic is indicated by the bishop's hat placed over the arms.

The Saldanha service must have been enormous. Even in its present incomplete state it numbers more than 200 pieces. It is by far the most colorful of all the McCann services, and its decoration is most unusual. Food, appropriately enough, is its theme. A ham furnishes the central motive, and in the surrounding field, ducks, fish, fruit, and vegetables are used decoratively. The border designs are based on types used in European ceramics. Specifically, the floral swags and ribbons are in style similar to those found on a Meissen plate of about 1760. The landscapes in the small cartouches in the border may be compared with those on the Holburn platter (Plate 36), also dated about 1760.

An unusual feature of the service is that it includes a number of plates and covers of enameled copper which were obviously painted by the very craftsmen responsible for the decoration of the Saldanha porcelains. This relationship between Cantonese enamels on copper and enameled porcelains was referred to in the last chapter of Part I.

Two fine examples of China-Trade porcelain of the sixties showing the rococo style of armorial decoration are a cup and saucer (Plate 39). Within the conjoined ovals, surrounded by coral-colored rococo framing and supported by the figures of Neptune and Venus, are the bust of a woman and a cipher. Neither the subject of the portrait nor the meaning of the cipher is known. The flag of Denmark flies from the mast of the ship in the saucer's border; we may be sure, therefore, that the cup and saucer were made for Danish use. That they, with their companion teapot (Fig. 40), date from the 1760s is indicated by comparison with a teapot in the possession of Mrs. Arthur A. Houghton, Jr., upon which the same type of shield, cipher, supporters, and border decoration are to be seen. The Houghton teapot bears the date 1763.

A richly adorned dinner service which possesses much the same style of rococo armorial decoration as the Danish cup and saucer—even the supporters are identical—was made at about the same time for the same market. The differences in armorial design are negligible. In place of a portrait and a cipher there are two ciphers, and these are on a blue, rather than on a white, ground. The border design for the service consists of blue and gold floral swags and a spearhead border (see Plate 41).

Outstanding in this service of more than 100 pieces is the tureen (Plate 40), which in the delicate rococo modeling of its gleaming white surface is a thing of exceptional charm. It is completely European in form. More than that, it is a copy after a pottery tureen (Fig. 41) made at the Höchst factory in Germany by Ignatz Hess, who was active there during the middle years of the century.

An especially pleasing example with armorial decoration of the sixties is found in the teapot which bears the Hayes arms and is richly colored in gold (Plate 4). There are few China-Trade teapots in any collection that can vie with this splendid example.

From Holland comes an admirable piece, a dish with an unusual border composed of European and Chinese motives (Plate 5). It is the work of Cantonese painters who seem to have followed as best they could the canons of rococo decoration, with curious and diverting results. The plate, incidentally, was once believed to have been made for Louis XV's favorite, Madame de Pompadour. Her coat of arms, however, is far from the one here shown, which belongs to the Dutch family of Snoeck. The tinctures are bright blue and gold; and there are a variety of brilliant hues in the border.

Among the other McCann porcelains of this period we illustrate several with rococo arms which remain unidentified. These were presumably made for the Continental market, for the arms differ in their make-up from those commonly used by English families. One of them, a plate (Plate 3), is a particularly splendid example of armorial decoration. The principal tinctures are black and gold. Three items from a coffee service (Plate 42) and three cups and a creamer (Plate 43) from various tea services may also be grouped together in the decade of the sixties. The teacups are characteristically Oriental in form; the other pieces are based on European ceramic prototypes.

PLATE 37 *Platter with the arms of Saldanha de Albuquerque. Portuguese market*

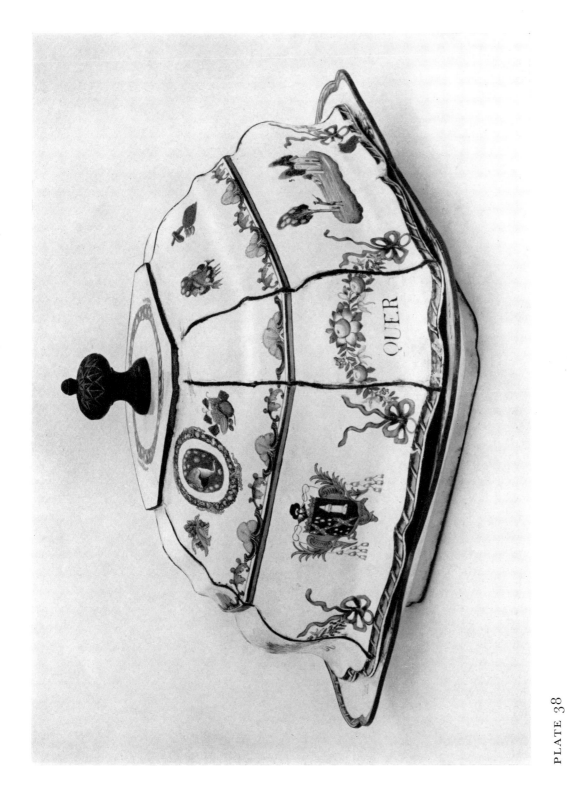

PLATE 38

Tray and cover of enameled copper with the arms of Saldanha de Albuquerque. Portuguese market 1760–1770

FIGURE 40 *China-Trade armorial porcelains made for the Danish market in the 1760s*

LEFT: Teapot bearing the date 1763. Collection of Mrs. Arthur A. Houghton, Jr., New York. RIGHT: Teapot with heraldic and border decorations resembling those on the Houghton teapot. (Shown also in Figure 34)

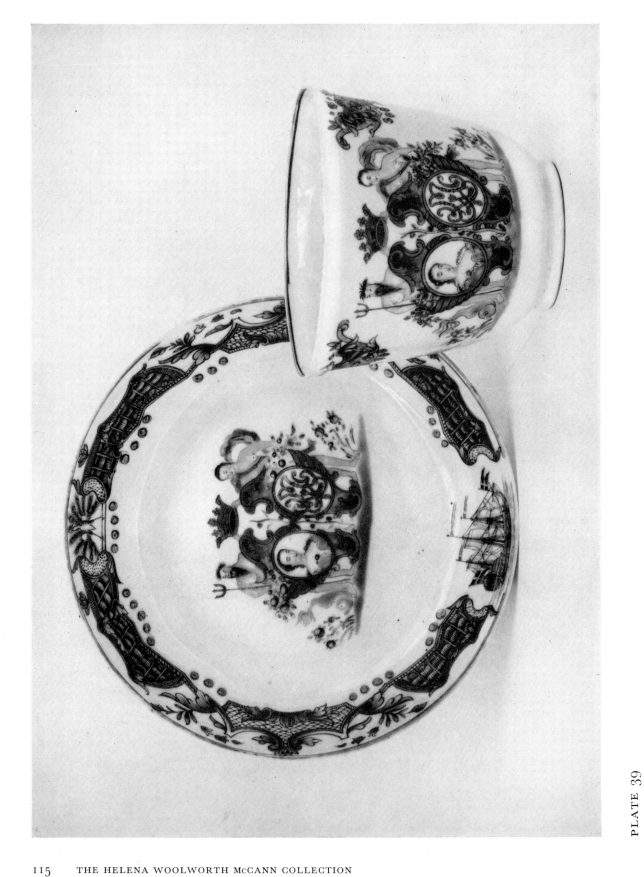

PLATE 39

Cup and saucer with two shields enclosing an unidentified portrait and cipher. Danish market

1760–1770

FIGURE 41

Pottery tureen made at the Höchst factory in Germany by Ignatz Hess between 1747 and 1751. Ex coll. Rosenheim, London

PLATE 40

Tureen with unidentified arms, after a pottery model from the Höchst factory. Danish market 1760–1770

PLATE 41

Plate with unidentified arms. Danish market

1760–1770

PLATE 42

Coffee pot, bowl, and sugar caster with unidentified arms. Continental market?
1760–1770

PLATE 43

Three teacups and a creamer with unidentified arms. Continental market?

1760–1770

PORCELAINS WITH
ARMORIAL DECORATIONS
1770–1785

A notable group of armorial porcelains may be dated towards the end of the 1740–1785 period. In examining these pieces we note that the baroque and rococo forms that had dominated heraldic delineation in the mid-eighteenth century have now given way to less elaborate styles. The spade-shaped shield appears. With this group it is more difficult than with the earlier porcelains to determine exactly the period of any particular piece. There are no "dated" pieces among them to guide us, and the evidence of decorative style, although helpful, is not explicit. It must be pointed out that some of these porcelains could have been made shortly after 1785, although, according to our interpretation of the evidence of style, this seems unlikely.

The McCann collection includes an impressive service made late in this period, probably before 1785, for a member of the Newman family. The tureen illustrated in Plate 44 is but one of more than 75 pieces from the service that are preserved in the collection. Except for its arms, which were enameled in full color at Canton, its decoration was completely carried out in underglaze blue at Chingtechen. Wide blue bands filled with an inconspicuous diaper pattern characterize the decoration. The bands are edged with a spear-head motive in underglaze blue and not in gold in the manner of the Cantonese painters. As here presented, the spear-head border had seen its best days, offering but a pale reflection of its former elegance.

Related in style and period to the Newman service is the tea set with the arms of the Griffiths family on a spade-shaped shield, beneath which is the Griffiths motto, FIDES NON TIMET (Plate 45). Here again are found the same underglaze blue bands and the same debased blue spear-head pendants. A secondary border consists of a narrow line of small dart-like elements, a motive which seems to have been in use before 1785. Since we will find the same dart-like border appearing on pieces made after 1785 (Plate 83), it is possible that the Griffiths porcelains belong to that later period, but the evidence does not warrant a certain attribution.

The teapot in the Griffiths service is an early example in China-Trade ware of that cylindrical type which in almost unvarying form continued to be produced for export during the latter years of the eighteenth century (see page 55). A Worcester teapot of 1765–1770 (Fig. 42) represents a possible Western ceramic prototype.

Of the great Gordon dinner and tea services, nearly 250 pieces are to be found in the McCann collection. To judge from the manner in which the arms are represented, these services were made before 1785.

Like the Newman service, which may be of a slightly earlier date, the Gordon services received the major part of their decoration at Chingtechen (Plates 7, 46–48). The elaborate underglaze blue border of the dinner service, of the type known as Fitzhugh, suggests a Chinese landscape with rocks, flowers, and butterflies (Plate 47). This pattern, of which the present example is an early version, continued to be used in ever more conventionalized form as late as the first half of the nineteenth century.

Another innovation may be observed in three dishes from the Gordon tea service (Plate 48): the fashion of decorating the borders of dishes with pierced work. Pierced work is, of course, characteristic of a number of Chinese porcelains

of the K'ang-hsi and Ch'ien Lung periods. The technique was adopted by the West and is to be found on Meissen and other porcelains. The form in which it is used by the Chingtechen makers of China-Trade porcelains, as exemplified by the Gordon dishes, derives not so much from Western adaptations as from Chinese porcelains themselves, another instance of Chinese decoration replacing Western decoration at this period.

The use of pierced work is seen again in a plate from the Grierson service (Plate 49), which is represented by more than 130 pieces in the McCann collection. It is clearly in the same style as the Gordon plates illustrated in Plate 48, and the Grierson arms are represented in much the same manner as those of the Gordon family: on spade-shaped shields within oval enframements. The outer border of the Grierson piece is decorated with a narrow scrolling foliate pattern in mauve and green. The smaller inner border in the form of a floral swag is also painted in mauve and green with the addition of red, which is the chief color of the shield.

The foliate border pattern of still another example of the armorial wares seemingly made prior to 1785, a covered chestnut dish of neoclassic design with unidentified arms (Plate 50), repeats a motive already observed on the Grierson service. The same colors—mauve and green—are used. Since the workmanship also seems to be identical, we may conclude that the chestnut dish and the Grierson service received their enamel decoration in the same Cantonese workshop at the same time.

An attractive dinner service bears in a plain oval shield arms which may be French (Plate

51), although the heraldic evidence is not complete enough to permit identification of the family to whom they belonged. It may be noted that the armorial enframement, although reminiscent of the earlier baroque style, is simplified in a manner not to be found in armorial decorations of the middle of the century.

This extensive service, of which the McCann collection includes more than 160 pieces, is strongly Western in decoration. The basketwork border, for example, is of a type which originated in Meissen in the 1730s and was later used in various other European porcelain centers. In Germany it was called the *alt-Ozier* pattern. There is, unfortunately, little in the way of other decorative detail to relate this service to the porcelains just described. We may, however, note the small dotted banding in underglaze blue along the edge of the border, an element which may be compared with similar bandings found on the Grierson pieces and on the chestnut dish. Such as they are, the indications suggest that the service with the supposed French arms, too, was made before 1785.

PLATE 44

Tureen with the Newman arms. English market

1770–1785

FIGURE 42

Worcester porcelain teapot. 1765–1770. Rous Lench collection, Evesham

PLATE 45

Selected pieces from a tea service with the Griffiths arms. English market
1770–1785

PLATE 46

Pitcher with the Gordon arms. English market

1770–1785

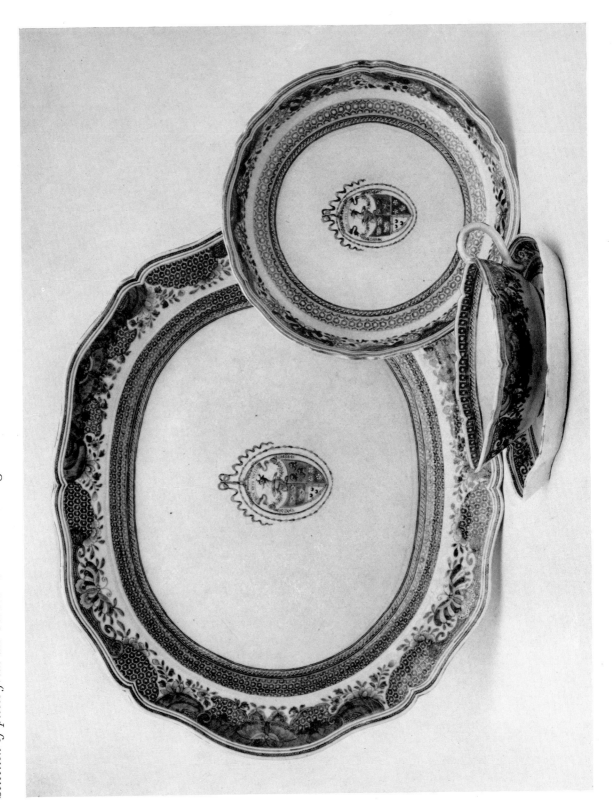

PLATE 47   1770–1785

Selection of pieces from the Gordon dinner service. English market

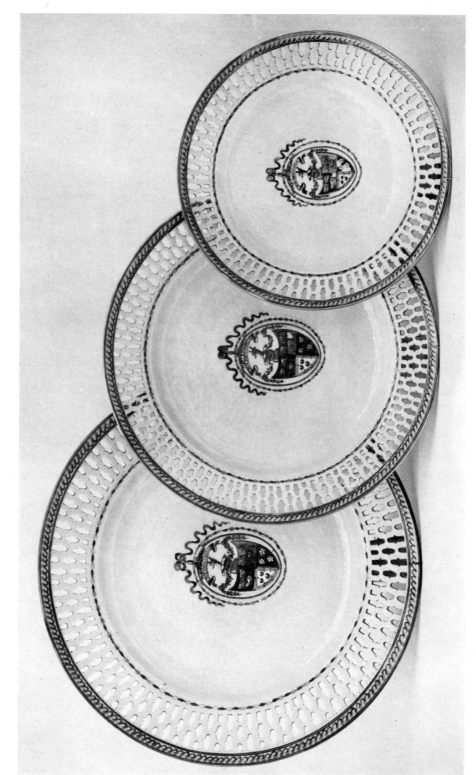

PLATE 48

1770–1785

Selection of plates from the Gordon tea service. English market

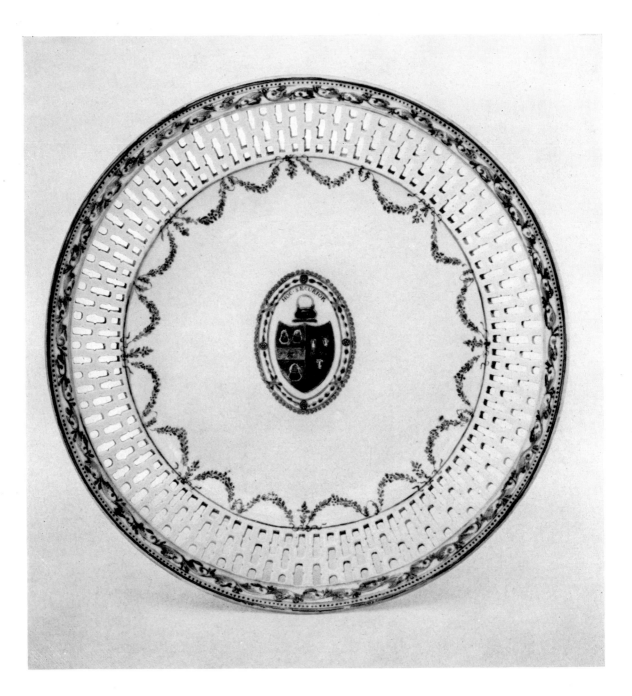

PLATE 49

Dish with the Grierson arms. English market
1770–1785

PLATE 50

Chestnut bowl and cover with unidentified arms. English market

1770–1785

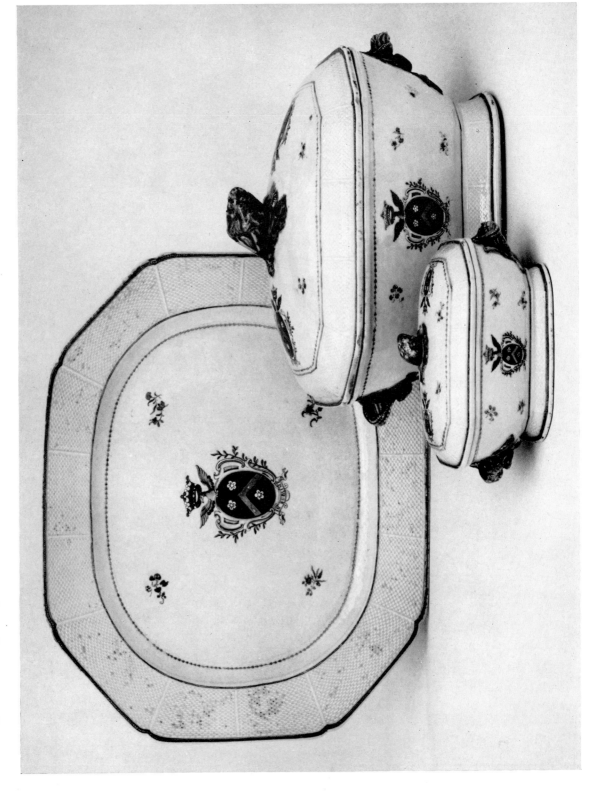

PLATE 51   *Selected pieces from a dinner service with unidentified arms.   French market.?*

PORCELAINS WITH
DECORATIONS BASED ON
EUROPEAN PRINTS OR DRAWINGS
1740–1785

The several pieces with religious subjects in the McCann collection date from a full half-century after Father d'Entrecolles's description of the type (see page 57). They also differ from his Crucifixion plate in that they were painted not in Chingtechen but at Canton. All are decorated in black on the white porcelain surface, and a number of them are surely after engravings. The Dutch ware that they resemble is represented in Figure 43.

Characteristic of the porcelains with religious decorations in the McCann collection are a cup, saucer, and creamer (Plate 52), each of which shows the Crucifixion—surely a strange subject for teatime. Both the composition and the technique used on them by the porcelain painter are seemingly reflections of some Western print, possibly one taken from a Bible. Another cup and saucer show the Resurrection (Plate 53), a composition repeated in a dish with an elaborate Western border (Plate 8). In the latter example the correspondence between the style of the Cantonese painters and the technique of the Western engravers is especially clear.

The Baptism of Christ as represented on a plate (Plate 54) is rendered more in the manner of a monochrome painting than a print. The Chinese artist's ignorance of both the meaning of the picture and Western conventions of perspective has produced a curious piece. Christ and Saint John look like two Chinese peasants deep in a rice paddy, and the dove of the Holy Ghost, instead of casting his rays upon the two figures, appears to be ascending directly into celestial space. Four fat and very Chinese winged putti appear in the pseudo-Western border. Drawn without understanding, a devotional picture has acquired a somewhat comic air.

Since specific models for none of these religious porcelains have been identified, the designs give us no precise idea as to when they were made. So we have to rely upon the evidence of border ornament. The Resurrection (Plate 8) and the Baptism of Christ (Plate 54) both have border designs which conform to styles current in European ceramic work of the mid-eighteenth century. The Resurrection cup and saucer (Plate 53) and the Crucifixion cup, saucer, and creamer (Plate 52) bear the spearhead border which, as has been indicated (page 58), is the mark of the mid-decades of the eighteenth century. Indeed, it seems likely that all the black-and-white pieces here described were painted in Canton between 1750 and 1770.

Turning now to the porcelains decorated with secular subjects, we find that a number of them also were painted in the manner of Western engravings. An outstanding example of this sort of work is a plate (Plate 55) the decoration of which copies a print, *Pèlerins de l'Isle de Cythère*, made in 1708 by Bernard Picart, an engraver of French origin active in the Netherlands (Fig. 44). It may be noted that the subject of the print itself is based on one of the ballets or operas popular in Paris early in the eighteenth century. From such a source Watteau was later inspired to create his famous composition *L'Embarquement pour Cythère*. That the China-Trade porcelain version of the subject was probably painted in the 1750s seems indicated by the shadowy remains of a white enamel border in the mid-century Meissen "lacework" style.

An amusing punch bowl (Plate 56) has as its chief decorative subject *The Concert*. A number of Europeans are shown in what seems to be an informal gathering of amateur musicians, a scene repeated on the bowl's opposite side. Between the two scenes a Chinese orchestra is represented in smaller scale. The four concerts are executed in black and white in the manner of an engraving. And appropriately so, for the model of the European subject is a print by an anonymous British artist of the mid-eighteenth century, an example of which is in the Metropolitan Museum (Fig. 45). The design of the Chinese concert may be of Oriental origin.

The areas around the concert scenes are richly worked in gold and enlivened by vignettes showing Chinese landscapes. The bowl's inner rim is decorated with a scrolling rococo border in gold that may be based on a European ceramic prototype. Since the very same style of

decoration occurs on a mug bearing the date 1758 (Plate 33), the punch bowl too was presumably made close to 1760.

A cup and saucer (Plate 57) decorated in black and white with scenes in which a lady on a doorstep converses with a gentleman represents a slightly later example of porcelain with designs from European prints or drawings. The costumes of the figures in the scene suggest that the subject is copied from a print, possibly one of Dutch origin, of the first half of the eighteenth century. Despite the fact that the pictorial decoration derives from an early period, the way in which the design is placed on the surfaces of cup and saucer and the use of a plain narrow banding for borders relate these porcelains to a cup and saucer of *The Tea Party* pattern, which, as we shall presently see (page 147), can be dated within the period of 1770–1785.

A tea service of which there are ten pieces in the McCann collection is painted in black on white in imitation of an engraving. Upon each is a medallion enclosing a representation of *The Embroideress* (Plates 9 and 58). The severity of the color scheme is mitigated by the fact that the seamstress's dress is painted in gold, a bright note effectively repeated in the spear-head border. As is usually the case, this narrow border is itself outlined in red.

Although the original model for *The Embroideress* composition remains unidentified, it seems to be Dutch in style. A simplified variant of the design is shown on the teapot at the right of Figure 34.

The vogue for decorating wares with pictorial subjects was not limited to black on white. Many subjects were reproduced in colors, and a number of brilliant examples are to be found in the McCann collection. Among these are a tureen and platter (Plate 10) from a dinner service represented in the collection by 16 pieces. They are amusingly decorated. Within their central medallions a hunter and his dog approach a lady seated under a tree. Above, a man peers out of the foliage. Whether the hunter has treed the man or whether the latter is spying on the couple below must remain a mystery until someone discovers the composition's origin. The border of purplish floral swags is similar to one already observed in the armorial tureen and monteith (Plates 29 and 30), which were ascribed to the 1750s—a dating equally applicable to the pieces considered here. The tureen's handles and the cover knob are painted in orange and gold.

An imposing punch bowl (Plate 59) may also be included in this group. Its subject is *Beating and Trailing for a Hare*, and here the source of the design is known: a colored mezzotint engraved by Burford after a composition by James Seymour and published in 1753. Although the print was republished in 1787, the presence of the spear-head border indicates that the original version of the print served as the model.

Other porcelains with pictorial decorations in color are two plates made between 1750 and 1770. The first has for its subject *The Cherry Pickers* (Plate 60), a composition based indirectly on Nicolas Lancret's *La Terre* as popularized through the engraving of C. N. Cochin. The second has for its central motive a portrait of a woman that in spirit recalls the work of Sir Joshua Reynolds (Plate 61). Its model may have been an engraving made after a painting.

Also to be mentioned are two plates with marine subjects (Plates 62 and 63), which on the evidence of their style and of the Dutch flag flying from ships figuring in their compositions were made either from drawings sent from Holland or from drawings made in Canton by gifted Hollanders engaged in the East India trade.

FIGURE 43

Delft pottery plate with a Crucifixion after an engraving by the Dutch master Merian. 1720–1730. A. Nijstad, The Hague

PLATE 52

Teacup, saucer, and creamer depicting the Crucifixion. Continental market 1750–1770

PLATE 53

Teacup and saucer depicting the Resurrection. Continental market?

1750–1770

PLATE 54

Plate depicting the Baptism of Christ. Continental market?

1750–1770

PLATE 55

Plate with the Pèlerins de l'Isle de Cythère, after an engraving by Bernard Picart. Dutch market?

1750–1760

FIGURE 44   *Pèlerins de l'Isle de Cythère*

Engraving made in 1708 by Bernard Picart, a French master active in Holland. M. E. Brunard collection, Brussels

FIGURE 45 *The Concert*

Engraving by an anonymous British artist. Mid-XVIII century. The Metropolitan Museum of Art

PLATE 56

Punch bowl with The Concert, after a print by an anonymous British artist. English market 1750–1760

PLATE 57

Cup and saucer showing a lady on a doorstep. Continental market?

1770–1785

PLATE 58

Selected pieces from a tea service with copies of *The Embroideress. Dutch market?*

1750–1770

PLATE 59

Punch bowl with a sporting scene after the mezzotint Beating and Trailing for a Hare, by Burford. English market

1755–1770

PLATE 60

Plate with the subject popularly known as The Cherry Pickers. *Continental market*

1750–1770

PLATE 61

Plate with a woman's portrait. English market?

1750–1770

PLATE 62

Plate with marine decoration. Dutch market

1750–1770

PLATE 63

Plate with marine decoration. Dutch market

1750–1770

Among the McCann porcelains with decorations based on European ceramic models are a tureen and platter (Plate 64) showing views of merchants at the water's edge, ships beyond, and, in the far distance, mountains. These porcelains are typical of a considerable group of China-Trade wares decorated with harbor scenes. So it is not surprising to find a variant of the same subject used on one of the teapots in the McCann collection (Fig. 34, left). In this instance a tower is an added feature of the design. And a similar water-front subject appears as a vignette in the border of the Holburn platter (Plate 36). It may be noted that the cartouches enclosing the Holburn vignettes are in shape almost the duplicates of those found on the tureen and platter.

Porcelains decorated with such harbor scenes were evidently based on ceramic models of the West, particularly those of Meissen. Possible Meissen prototypes, such as those shown in Figure 46, were manufactured between 1730 and 1740. The China-Trade tureen and platter (Plate 64) are later—I place them between 1750 and 1760—for there was sometimes a considerable time-lag between the appearance of a decorative convention in Europe and its application to porcelain in Canton. However, they seem no later than the stylistically related Holburn platter referred to above, which has been dated about 1760.

Related to the wares decorated with harbor scenes is a plate which shows a road along a rugged shore (Plate 65). Although the original for this landscape is not known, the nature of its subject, its ornamental framework, and the border, all suggest that the plate is a copy after or an adaptation from a European ceramic model.

Three pieces from a tea service (Plate 66, below) furnish yet other examples of China-Trade porcelain with decorations from a European source. Although again the exact model is unknown, the *Venus and Cupid* which is painted on them in bright reds and greens is surely close to the subject appearing on a Meissen bowl of about 1745 (Fig. 47). Closely related to the *Venus and Cupid* porcelains are the cup and saucer from a tea service which shows a similar mythological subject: *Venus and Mercury* (Plate 66, above).

A design known as the Valentine pattern appears in a number of English ceramic wares of the eighteenth century. One of them is a Worcester teapot of about 1760 (see Fig. 48). The Valentine pattern consists of three motives, all of them, naturally, of a sentimental nature. There is the altar upon which two hearts are impaled by Cupid's darts; the "Tree of Golden Apples"; and the pair of lovebirds perched upon a bow and quiver.

This amusing design is also found on a China-Trade mug (Plate 67). In the Oriental version one heart upon the altar takes the place of two, and the tree does not bear golden apples as it should (see Fig. 48). The lovebirds are, however, correctly perched upon a bow and quiver. The mug may be dated 1760–1770 and seems to have been made for the English market.

A platter (Plate 68) having a central field decorated with fruits, vegetables, and flowers presents a Cantonese version of a widely used European ceramic design. It is part of a large dinner service. A characteristic Western example of this composition appears on a pottery plate made at the Künersberg manufactory in Germany in 1760 (Fig. 49). The Chinese version, although probably later, may still have been made in the sixties, when this design was at the height of its popularity in the West.

A connection with the ceramic styles of the West is clearly evident in a cup and saucer (Plate 69, above). Their decoration is a familiar English porcelain design known in both Worcester and Bow china as *The Tea Party*. Robert Hancock designed the composition in the third quarter of the eighteenth century, and his name appears on a Worcester cup on which this decoration occurs (Fig. 50). The only significant difference between the Worcester and the Canton versions lies in the kind of tea table represented. The table in the English piece is Georgian in style; the one in the Canton porcelain is Oriental. English wares with this subject may be variously dated in the sixties and the seventies. The cup and saucer in the McCann collection were presumably made for the English market at a time when this pattern was still in the mode. Between 1770 and 1785 seems to be a reasonable date for them.

Another cup and saucer (Plate 69, below) may be grouped with the example of *The Tea Party*. These show a man and woman seated under a tree, with two children at the woman's side. This type of subject, of unknown origin, was repeated many times on English wares.

A cup and saucer made in the late years of this period have chinoiserie decoration (Plate 70, above). Although the figures are Chinese, they seem to follow a Western model. Since chinoiserie decorations are frequently met with in English porcelains of the second half of the eighteenth century, it may be presumed that the model was some such porcelain from England. The McCann cup and saucer may therefore be a Chinese interpretation of an English interpretation of a Chinese porcelain design. The relation of the design to the porcelain areas and the use of a narrow linear edging indicate that these pieces were made at about the time of *The Tea Party* cup and saucer—that is, between 1770 and 1785.

Also of this period is the small covered cup (Plate 70, below) showing a view of Roman ruins. No ceramic model for it is known, but the sure manner in which the decoration covers the cup's entire surface suggests that the design stems from a painted ceramic model rather than from a print. This skillful adaptation of decoration to shape may be contrasted with the lack of imagination often shown in the handling of subjects based on a print or drawing; for example, the way the ship is placed on the Sousa platter (Plate 92). It is to be noted that the cover's narrow linear edging is nearly the same as that on the chinoiserie cup and saucer.

FIGURE 46 *Meissen porcelains with harbor scenes*
ABOVE: Teapot. 1730–1735. Cecil Higgins Museum, Bedford, England. BELOW: Bowl. About 1740. Ex coll. W. W. Winkworth. Beauchamp Galleries, London

PLATE 64

Tureen and platter with a harbor scene. Continental—possibly Danish—market
1750–1760

PLATE 65

Plate with a landscape decoration. Continental market

1750–1770

FIGURE 47 *Bowl with Venus and Cupid decoration*

Meissen porcelain painted in the workshop of J. F.
Metzsch, Bayreuth, about 1745. British Museum

PLATE 66

Above: *Cup and saucer from a tea service with Venus and Mercury. Continental market*
Below: *Selected pieces from a tea service with Venus and Cupid. Continental market*

1750-1770

FIGURE 48 *The Altar of Love*
 Worcester teapot with this decoration. About
1760. Ex coll. Mrs. Willoughby Hodgson

PLATE 67

Mug with an Altar of Love. English market
1760–1770

PLATE 68

*Platter with fruit decoration.
Continental market*

1760–1770

FIGURE 49

Pottery plate made at the Künersberg manufactory
in Germany about 1760. Igo Levi collection, Lucerne

FIGURE 50

Worcester porcelain bowl decorated with *The Tea Party*, a composition by Robert Hancock. About 1760. The Metropolitan Museum of Art

PLATE 69

Above: *Cup and saucer with The Tea Party, after a design by Robert Hancock. English market*

Below: *Cup and saucer. English market?*

1770–1785

PLATE 70

Above: *Cup and saucer with chinoiserie decoration. Continental market?*
Below: *Cup and cover decorated with a scene of Roman ruins. Continental market*

1770–1785

PORCELAINS WITH
FORMS BASED ON
EUROPEAN CERAMIC MODELS
1740–1785

Specific evidence concerning the influence of Western ceramic forms on China-Trade porcelains may be offered. First we present a jardinière modeled and painted in the rococo style in gold and rich Chinese red-orange (Plate 11). It follows closely, in both form and decoration, a jardinière made between 1758 and 1766 at the Marieberg factory near Stockholm (Fig. 51). Just as the European model almost certainly was carried to Canton in a ship of the Swedish East India Company, the Chinese version of it would seem to have been sent westwards under the same auspices for the Swedish market.

Other examples include two armorial porcelains already described as based on European ceramic models: the tureen (Plate 40) which belongs to a service made for the Danish market during the 1760s and a teapot (Plate 45) bearing the Griffiths arms and possibly made before 1785. Two pairs of urns and a cress basket, soon to be described in detail (Plates 74 and 75, above), also have close parallels in European ceramics.

Although their models cannot be identified, the following pieces also seem to belong to this group of porcelains based on Western ceramic models: a watch stand (Plate 71), a tureen in the form of a goose (Plate 72), and perhaps a figure of a dog and a covered dish in the form of a fish (Plate 73).

The applied molded decoration of floral sprays on the watch stand represents a Chinese porcelain technique that had been adopted by Europeans, but in this instance it is presumably based on a European version. Tureens in the form of water fowl were common in eighteenth-century Europe, as were ceramic figures of animals. There is, however, no mistaking the place of origin of the goose tureen or the dog, for Chinese craftsmen have endowed them with a thoroughly Oriental character.

Two pairs of handsome urns in the McCann collection are based on models from the Swedish factory at Marieberg.

One pair (see Plate 74, left) is painted in blue and white with details in gold. The model was made at Marieberg in 1773 (Fig. 52). No trace of late eighteenth-century Cantonese decoration is to be found on these porcelains, and it may be assumed that they were made during the decade following 1773.

The other pair of urns, of the pistol-handled variety (see Plate 74, right), seems to be somewhat freely based on a Marieberg flint porcelain model (Fig. 53) upon which is painted a portrait of Gustavus III of Sweden. The Marieberg piece, a characteristic example of the Gustavian style, was made about 1775. Adaptations of the pistol-handled urn proved so popular that this Swedish form continued to be manufactured in China as late as the 1790s, as we know from numerous examples directed to the American market. The pair of urns in the McCann collection seem to be fairly early examples of the type.

The cress basket (Plate 75, above) is a faithful copy of a pearlware basket made in Josiah Wedgwood's factory (Fig. 54) and dated "about 1780." The China-Trade version differs from the Wedgwood model only in the addition of a copy of Bartolozzi's stipple engraving of *Autumn* (Fig. 55).

The same subject appears on a companion porcelain, a covered chestnut dish (Plate 75, below). In addition to the pictorial decoration, details of the print's surrounding ornament—the work of Pergolesi—are also to be found on the chestnut dish. This dish also is evidently of Western ceramic form, although the actual model is unknown.

Bartolozzi's *Autumn*, which is after Cipriani's design, was published by Pergolesi in London in 1782, and the China-Trade versions of it may have been executed within the next few years, at a time when the design would still have been a novelty.

FIGURE 51 *Jardinières, model and copy*

ABOVE: Jardinière made at the Marieberg factory, Sweden, between 1758 and 1766. Vestlandske Kunst-industrimuseum, Bergen. BELOW: China-Trade jardinière based on the Marieberg model. 1760–1770. (Shown in color in Plate 11)

PLATE 71

Watch stand. Continental market?

1750–1770

PLATE 72

Tureen in the form of a goose. Continental market?

1750–1770

PLATE 73

Figure of a dog and a covered dish in the form of a fish. Continental market?

1750–1770

FIGURE 52

Pottery urn made at Marieberg, Sweden, in 1773.
Joseph Sachs collection, Stockholm

FIGURE 53

Flint porcelain urn made at Marieberg, Sweden,
about 1775. Niles Quist collection, Stockholm

PLATE 74

Left: *Urn after a pottery model first executed at the Marieberg factory in 1773. One of a pair. Swedish market*

Right: *Pistol-handled urn after a porcelain model first executed at the Marieberg factory about 1775. One of a pair. Swedish market?*

1775–1785

FIGURE 54

Wedgwood pearlware basket. About 1780. The Metropolitan Museum of Art

FIGURE 55 *Autumn*

Stipple engraving by Bartolozzi after Cipriani, published by Pergolesi, London, 1782. The Metropolitan Museum of Art

PLATE 75

Cress basket (above) *and chestnut dish and cover* (below), *each with a copy of Autumn, after a stipple engraving by Bartolozzi. English market*   ABOUT 1785

PORCELAINS WITH DECORATIONS PREDOMINANTLY CHINESE IN CHARACTER

1740–1785

Included in this final group of works of the 1740–1785 period are two characteristic *famille rose* porcelains which are perhaps more closely related to the Ch'ien Lung wares than to those of Europe. One, a plate, has a rose for its central theme (Plate 76). The design of the other, a punch bowl, centers upon a lush peony blossom (Plate 77). The bowl's divided ancestry is revealed by the border on its inner edge. Such borders are surely based on the types found on Meissen wares of the second quarter of the century; as we have already seen (page 132), these were used by the Cantonese during the third quarter of the century as the basis for various border designs.

Outstanding among the McCann porcelains that were made in the Chinese taste are two large punch bowls, each measuring more than twenty inches in diameter. Such bowls must have been a source of wonder in the West, for even after European ceramists had learned how to make porcelain, pieces of such vast proportions remained beyond the range of their abilities. One of the bowls (Plate 12) is decorated in gay colors, green and gold predominating, with a scene of Chinese peasants astride water buffalo. The other (Plate 78) shows within a large medallion, repeated four times on the vessel's side, lotus sprays in red, brown, and gold. These medallions are set against heavy petal designs in pastel shades of green, purple, blue, and rose. The bowl shows border designs within the rim and around the foot; a similar elaborate border is found on the inner rim of the bowl with the water buffalo scene.

The two bowls must be counted as exceptions to our account of the usual manner of producing porcelains for the Western market. Although they were clearly made for export—the punch bowl had no place in Chinese life—their painted decorations show no obvious trace of Western influence such as we would expect to find on porcelains painted at Canton. Moreover, their painting is more proficient than that found on any of the pieces so far examined, all of which, of course, were decorated at Canton. In both style and technique these punch bowls have much more in common with porcelains decorated at Chingtechen for Chinese use, and it may be concluded that they were painted not in Canton but in Chingtechen.

As has already been pointed out, it is always difficult to date purely Chinese porcelains with any degree of exactitude. The same holds for the two punch bowls. Although their designs recall those of the Yung Chêng period (1723–1735), they may be somewhat later. As a guess, it seems reasonable to assign them to the third quarter of the eighteenth century. It is, on the other hand, always possible that they may be of a prior date. Of the two, the one with the Chinese peasants would seem to be the earlier.

PLATE 76

Plate with rose decoration. Continental market?

1750–1770

PLATE 77

Punch bowl with peony decoration. Continental market?

1750–1770

PLATE 78

Punch bowl with lotus decoration Continental market

1750–1775

PORCELAINS OF
1785-1820

In the 1785–1820 period two contrary trends may be observed in the form and decoration of China-Trade porcelains.

There was, on the one hand, the impulse to continue along the lines that had hitherto been followed with such success during the 1740–1785 period; that is, to work in a close approximation of European styles. The Silveira service (Plates 15, 81, and 82), as we shall see, exemplifies this tendency.

The other impulse was towards an orientalization of design. This tendency, as we have already suggested, seems to have developed with the decline of the porcelain trade and was to prove the stronger of the two. Although Oriental details were, of course, almost never entirely absent from any example of China-Trade ware, their use increased steadily during the period from 1785 to 1820. By the end of the period the typical pieces made for export were predominantly Chinese in character, as can be seen from a study of the following pieces in the McCann collection.

PORCELAINS WITH ARMORIAL DECORATIONS 1785–1820

A number of the McCann porcelains, by the manner in which their coats of arms, ciphers, or ornamental decorations have been delineated, seem to have been made between 1785 and 1800. Among them are 100 pieces from a dinner and tea service which bear the Hammond arms on a spade-shaped shield (Plates 14 and 79). This service is richly effective in its coloration of sepia and brown, enhanced by gilded borders containing cartouches framing Chinese landscapes.

The Hammond service is surely not much later than the chestnut bowl (Plate 50) which has been dated before 1785. On the other hand, it shows close affinities to pieces which, on the evidence of ornamental detail later to be referred to, seem to have been made during the last fifteen years of the century. Particularly, it is closely associated in style with an armorial dinner service made for the Portuguese market (see Plate 80). This fine set bears the arms of Araujo de Acebedo and contains within double borders cartouches almost identical in form and placement to those on the Hammond service. In both instances the cartouches frame Chinese landscapes. That the Hammond and Araujo de Acebedo services, made respectively for the British and Portuguese markets, should be so similarly decorated suggests that they are of the same period. The manner in which the Araujo de Acebedo arms are represented may at first prove confusing, for it is reminiscent of a style of a half-century before. But, as we shall presently see from other instances, the Portuguese seem to have been more conservative than most Europeans when it came to changing their heraldic styles.

The lovely orange and gold armorial dinner service made for a member of the Silveira family of Portugal (Plates 15, 81 and 82) also belongs to this group of porcelains. It is one of the most brilliant services in the entire collection. The handsome arms on it are said to be those of Bernardo José Maria de Lorena e Silveira, fifth Count of Sarzedas, who was Portuguese Viceroy in India during the late eighteenth century. The border motive of crossed branches, which adds much to the decorative effect of the service, derives from Western ceramic ornament, although the exact model is not known.

A significant development to be noted in the decoration of these porcelains is the use of an entirely new variety of tiny ornamental borders or bandings, chiefly composed of dotted fillings within interlaced compartments. It occurs in the Araujo de Acebedo service where it defines the central field of a platter and rack (Plate 80). It appears also, in simpler form, on the Silveira service (Plates 15 and 82) and on a platter, to be described later, which memorializes the death of Louis XVI and his family in 1793 (Plate 90). A variation of it is to be found in the G. P. C. service (Plate 85, above), which, on the basis of

other evidence, can be dated towards the century's end.

From the armorial style and other evidences of date with which it is associated, this dotted banding may be taken as an indication of late eighteenth-century workmanship. It is this circumstance that prompts us to conclude that the Araujo de Acebedo, Silveira, and G. P. C. services, which bear such decorations, and the Hammond service, which is so closely related through other elements of ornament to the Araujo de Acebedo service, were all made during the period of 1785–1800.

On the basis of heraldic style, the sauce boat and tray with the arms of the Bruce family (Plate 83) may be placed after 1785. The shapes of both boat and tray are distinctive and are based on European ceramic forms. Although no exact model for either is known, similar trays with molded shell-shaped ornament in relief are found among Chelsea porcelains of the third quarter of the eighteenth century.

A date after 1785 may be given to the large covered cup with the cipher and crest of Peter Le Mesurier, Hereditary Governor of Alderney, who died in 1805 (Plate 84). The Le Mesurier cipher and crest are placed within a circular frame composed of tiny darts—a motive which had been in use even before 1785 (see Plate 45). As used here, this enframement is the same as that surrounding the Bruce arms on the sauce boat and tray (Plate 83). Further indication for the dating of the cup comes from the interlaced border design encircling the edge, a motive very similar to one on a coffee pot (Plate 100) made for the American market during the last decade of the century.

Two important armorial services in the Mc-Cann collection exemplify various characteristics of the late period of China-Trade porcelain. One is decorated with the initials G. P. C. on spade-shaped shields (Plate 85, above). The other shows the initials J.A. within oval medallions (Plate 85, below). On both services typical bandings of the period complete the decoration. The G. P. C. service has bandings with dotted fillings. On the J.A. service there is a blue band sown with gold stars, a motive that proved particularly popular with American buyers at Canton during the century's last decade.

The tureens in both services are almost identical in shape. This shape, which also occurs in the Silveira service, is noteworthy in that it occurs frequently in China-Trade services made late in the eighteenth century. Its form is rather massive, and it has interlaced handles. The tureen's most striking feature, however, is the knob on the cover—a hardy flower on a short stem that springs from a base of leaves. The knob is the clue to the origin of the tureens' design. An almost identical knob and somewhat the same type of handles appear on a similarly shaped creamware tureen (Fig. 56) illustrated as design number 4 in the Wedgwood catalogue for the year 1774. This was evidently a stock Wedgwood model, for it appeared again in the 1817 catalogue. Although used as early as 1774 in England, its influence on China-Trade porcelain is only discernible towards the end of the century. An export tureen of this type, published by Tudor-Craig in his *Armorial Porcelain* (p. 81), bears the arms of Van Notten-Pole impaling Buller. The service to which this piece belonged was probably ordered on the occasion of the marriage of Charles Van Notten-Pole to Felizarda Matilda Buller in 1795. The resemblance of the two McCann tureens to this one suggests that they also were made during the decade of 1790–1800.

A green and gold covered bowl (Plate 86) has the flamboyant appearance of many of the wares produced for the Portuguese market. The arms, those of Castro surmounted by a bishop's hat, confirm the association with Portugal and help to date the piece, for they belong to Don Antonio José de Castro, who was Bishop of Oporto from 1798 to 1814 and also Patriarch of Lisbon. In form and decoration the bowl was evidently inspired by a model of the Sèvres type.

The three armorial plates in Plate 87 are in the Portuguese taste. One, in the center, is from the Castro service, represented in Plate 86. The plate to the left of it appears from its heraldic style to have been made for a member of a Portuguese or, possibly, a Spanish family. To the right is a plate in orange and gold bearing the arms of Portugal. The inscription PALACIO DO GOVERNO DE MACAU indicates where the plate was originally used. Surely no more evocative provenance for a piece of China-Trade porcelain could be imagined than the palace of the Portuguese Governor of Macao. These last two plates, like the porcelains from the Castro service to which they are related in style, date from the first decade of the nineteenth century.

PLATE 79

Hot-water dish with the Hammond arms. English market

1785–1800

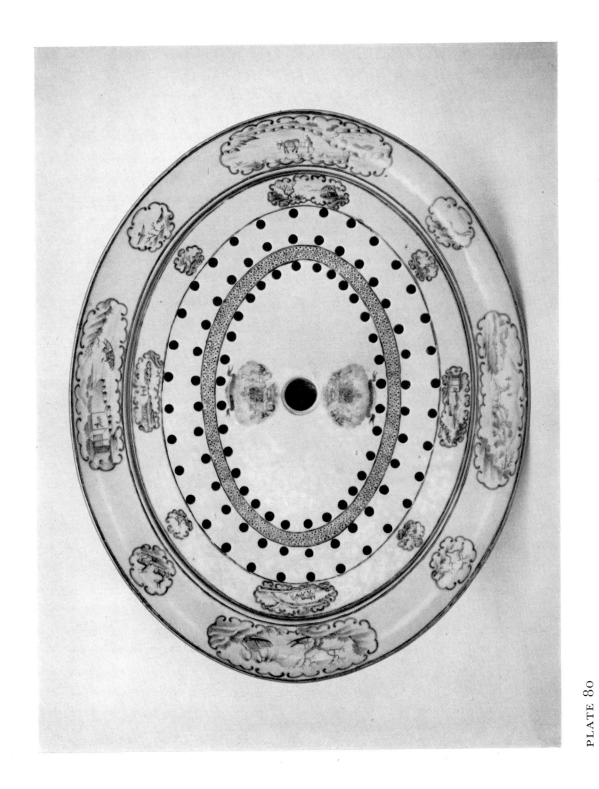

PLATE 80

Platter with rack, with the arms of Araujo de Acebedo. Portuguese market

1785–1800

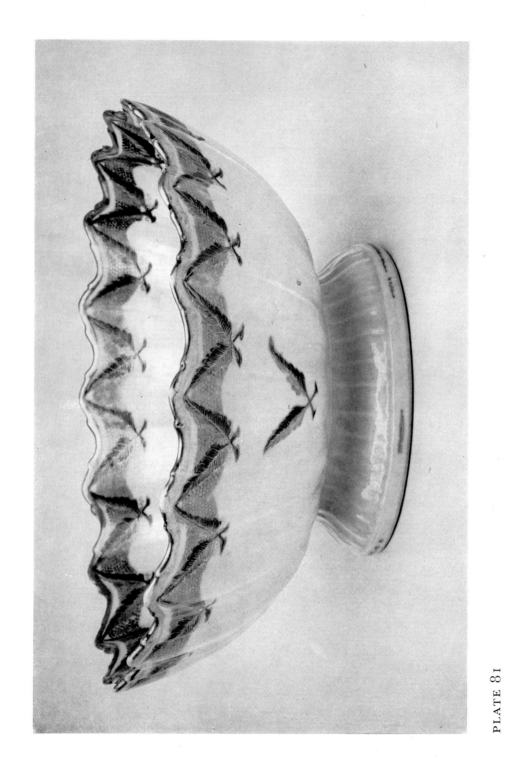

PLATE 81

Bowl with the arms of Silveira impaling Tavora. Portuguese market
1785–1800

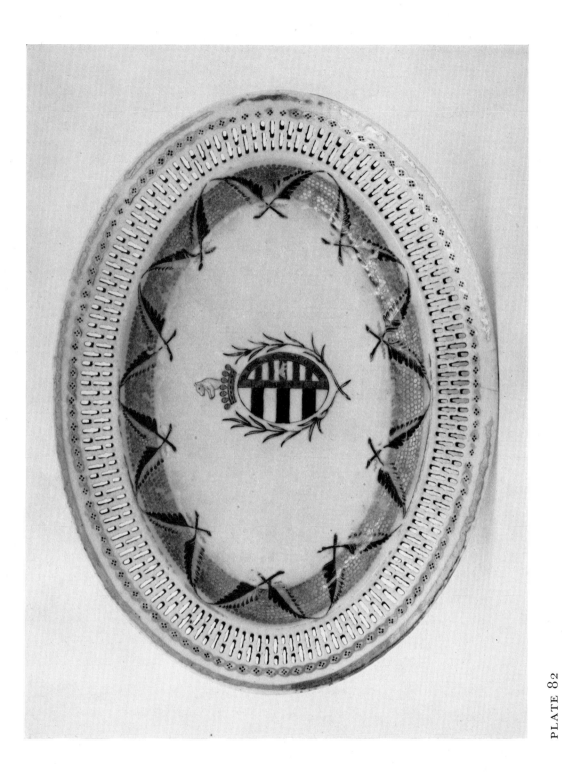

PLATE 82

Platter with the arms of Silveira impaling Tavora. Portuguese market

1785–1800

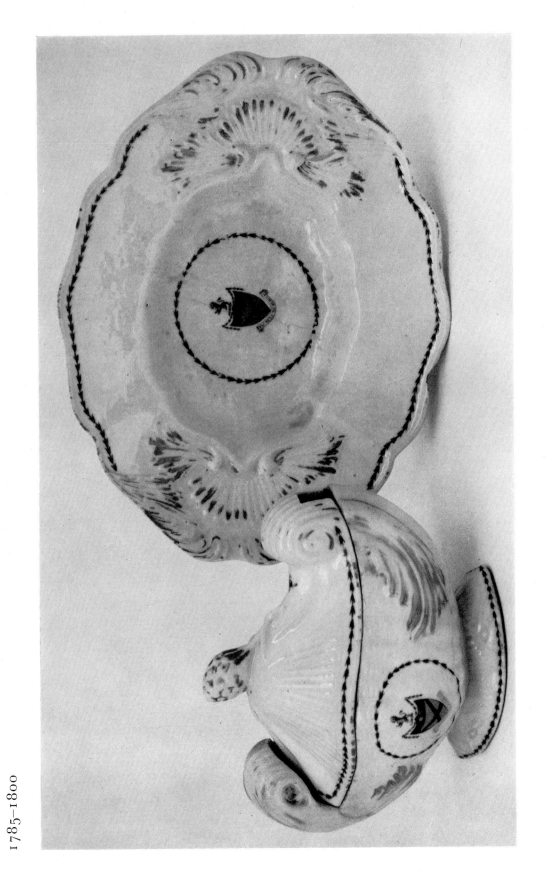

PLATE 83

Sauce boat and tray with the Bruce arms. English market

1785–1800

PLATE 84

Covered cup with the crest and initials of Peter Le Mesurier, Hereditary Governor of Alderney. English market

1785–1800

FIGURE 56

Creamware tureen shown in Wedgwood's 1774 catalogue

PLATE 85

Above: *Tureen and platter with the monogram G.P.C. English market*

Below: *Tureen and platter with the monogram J.A. English market*

1790–1800

PLATE 86

*Covered bowl with the arms of
Don Antonio José de Castro,
Bishop of Oporto from 1798 to
1814, and Patriarch of Lisbon.
Portuguese market*

1800–1810

PLATE 87

Left: *Plate with unidentified arms. Portuguese (or Spanish) market*

Center: *Plate with the Castro arms. Portuguese market*

Right: *Plate with the arms of Portugal and the inscription:* PALACIO DO GOVERNO DE MACAU. *Portuguese market*

1800–1810

PORCELAINS WITH DECORATIONS BASED ON EUROPEAN PRINTS OR DRAWINGS 1785–1820

Two punch bowls offer fine examples of the use of Western designs for the decoration of late China-Trade wares. One (Plate 13) shows farm boys at work; the other (Plate 88) illustrates an incident in a fox hunt. Like the pieces described in the preceding section, these seem to have been made between about 1785 and the century's end.

Their pictorial decorations are evidently based on European prints, although the actual source has not been found for either of them. Both show inside the rims the same plain wide borders which seem to be a characteristic of the late China-Trade style. Punch bowls with similar wide borders, for example, are illustrated by Jourdain and Jenyns, who assign them to the second half of the eighteenth century. They may well have been painted after 1785. One of the punch bowls, showing a rider on a pack horse, has the figure "79" on the packs. If the number stands for 1779, it might indicate the date of the print on which the design of the punch bowl is based.

The inner border of the punch bowl with a scene from a fox hunt (Plate 88) is further enriched by the addition of lacework edging. In contrast with the lacework borders in the Meissen manner used in Canton during the mid-eighteenth century (see Plates 55 and 77), this edging is curiously Chinese in detail. The precise manner in which the flowers are drawn in miniature and the circles are formed by a series of dots suggests that the lacework pattern conforms to the late eighteenth-century Cantonese style of draughtsmanship.

Among the porcelains of this group is a curiously decorated punch bowl (Plate 89) containing within a flower-bordered circular medallion a caricature of England's erratic monarch George III. From his mouth, as in a comic strip, issue the words: FOR · FOLLY · GEORGE · CHEAP · IS · MY · NAME · HA · HA · HA. George's parsimoniousness was one of the standard jokes of the period, as was his habit, whenever he felt he had scored a point, of haw-hawing. George III was the subject of a number of caricatures drawn by Gillray and others, especially during the last decade of the century. The one on the punch bowl seems typical of the lot.

A punch bowl in the Peabody Museum at Salem, painted in 1786 with a representation of Elias Hasket Derby's famous ship the *Grand Turk*, shows around its foot a banding of darts similar to that on the George III bowl. Various other bowls of the late eighteenth century show the same banding. Although we cannot determine exactly when the McCann example was made, the dates 1785–1800 should serve for it.

A platter of the same period as the George III punch bowl is decorated with a medallion in the center of which are placed a large urn and two willow trees (Plate 90). Nearly concealed within the outlines of the urn and the overhanging branches are silhouettes of Louis XVI, Marie Antoinette, and their children. The origin of this composition is to be found in a French engraving romantically called *L'Urne mystérieuse* (Fig. 57), published for royal sympathizers following the execution of the royal family in 1793. The platter's narrow, dotted border pattern is similar to those we have already seen in the McCann collection on various armorial porcelains of the late eighteenth century.

The last two pieces in this group are a punch bowl and a platter. The bowl (Plate 91) is decorated with a ship—possibly an American vessel, for its vaguely drawn flag seems to be that of the United States. The border design is entirely un-Western in detail—evidence, as we have already indicated, of a late date for China-Trade wares. The platter (Plate 92), which is from a large service now in the Henry Francis duPont Winterthur Museum, also has a ship for its central design. On the vessel's pennant are the initials M.A.S., which are believed to stand for Miguel Alvez Sousa, a shipowner of Macao. The platter is traditionally said to have formed part of a service which saw use on the very ship portrayed upon the porcelain, the *Brilliante*, which plied between Macao and Lisbon. The platter's meander border design, it will be noted, is undeviatingly Chinese. Although it is impossible to be precise about the dating of the platter—or of the punch bowl—the decade of 1800–1810 is suggested as the period during which they were made.

PLATE 88

Punch bowl with an incident in a fox hunt. English market?

1785–1800

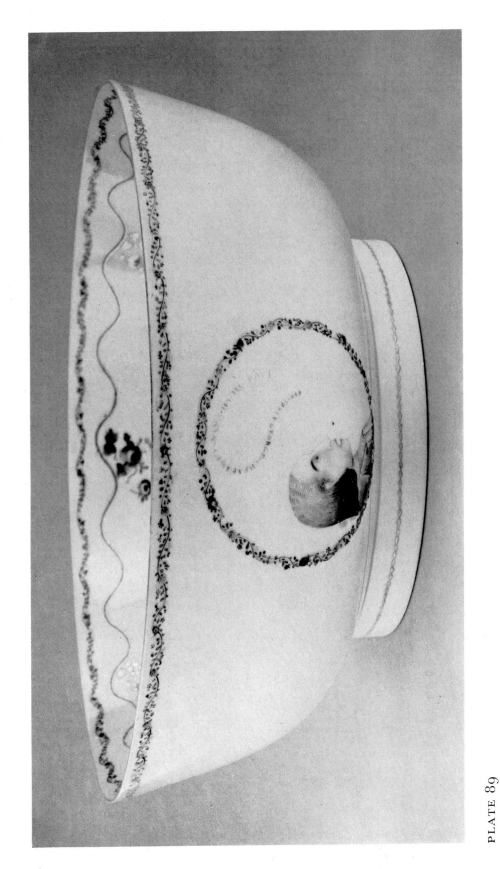

PLATE 89

Punch bowl with a caricature of George III. English market

1785–1800

FIGURE 57 *L'Urne mystérieuse*

Print published as a memorial to Louis XVI and his family. French, 1793–1800

PLATE 90

Platter made as a secret memorial to Louis XVI and his family. French market

1795–1800

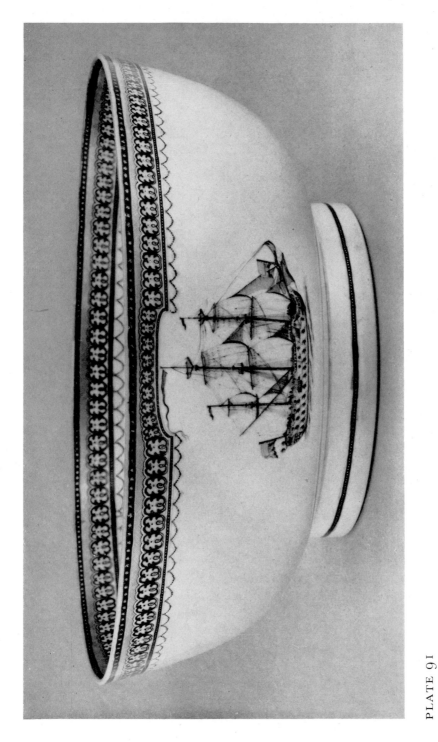

PLATE 91

Punch bowl with a China-Trade ship. European (or American) market　1800–1810

PLATE 92

Platter with a ship belonging to Miguel Alves Sousa of Macao. Portuguese market　1800–1810

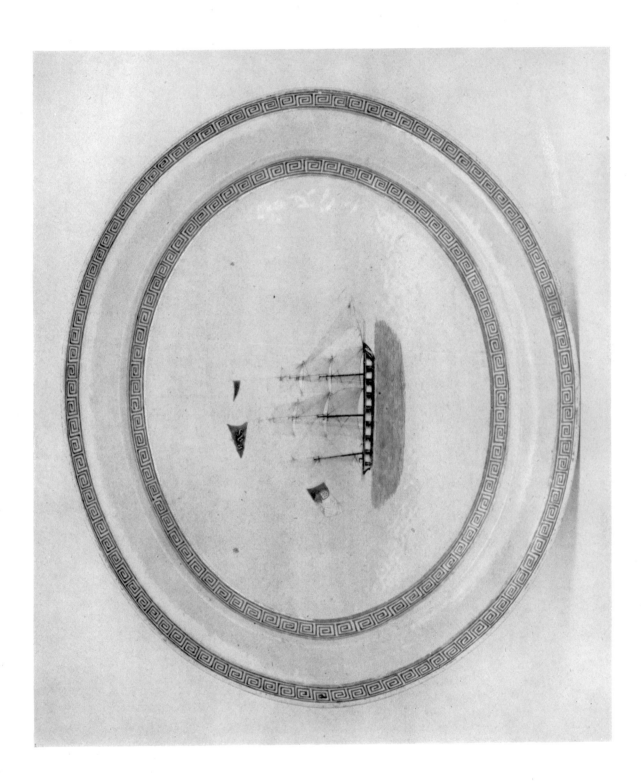

PORCELAINS WITH DECORATIONS BASED ON EUROPEAN CERAMIC MODELS 1785–1820

There are indications that three pieces in the 1785–1820 group were inspired by Western ceramic models. One is a platter (Plate 93), the yellow center of which is painted in the Chinese manner with feigned cracks. Sprays of flowers, symmetrically arranged in the Western manner, complete the central decoration. The border's dotted banding conforms to the Chinese type already met with in various late eighteenth-century pieces. Specifically, it may be compared with the border shown on the platter in Plate 90.

The two other examples, from a dinner service the design of which features a cornucopia motive, are a tureen and platter (Plates 94 and 95). Both pieces show an interweaving border design similar to a type appearing in late eighteenth-century English ceramics; for example, on a New Hall porcelain mug, dated 1785–1790. That the border design shown on the two China-Trade examples is an adaptation from some such model is evident from the presence of the meander motive, one of the elements of Oriental decoration frequently to be seen in Chinese export porcelain of the end of the eighteenth century.

It may be pointed out that the side and lid handles of the tureen are also based on European forms. Such handles were used in Germany as early as 1765–1770 at the Criseby and Eckernförde pottery works, and presumably elsewhere as well.

PLATE 93

Platter decorated with floral sprays. Continental market?

1790–1800

PLATE 94

Tureen with flower and cornucopia decoration. English market?
1790–1800

PLATE 95

Platter with flower and cornucopia decoration. English market?

1790–1800

PORCELAINS WITH
DECORATIONS PREDOMINANTLY
CHINESE IN CHARACTER
1785–1820

A considerable number of pieces in the McCann collection (of which only a few can be illustrated) show that the decorative forms of China became an increasingly significant element in the design of porcelain of the latest phase of the China Trade. A curious fruit basket on a stand (Plate 96) is perhaps the most European of the porcelains illustrated in this group. Although both basket and stand were surely inspired by Western ceramic prototypes, the stand as copied and painted by the artisans of Chingtechen is thoroughly Chinese in appearance and is, moreover, capped by an edging in the Chinese meander pattern.

Various versions of this type of fruit basket are known, one of which, a somewhat earlier piece in the Henry Francis duPont Winterthur Museum, bears the monogram of Major Samuel Shaw, who reached Canton in 1784 aboard the *Empress of China*. It also bears the badge of the Order of the Cincinnati, of which Shaw was a member (see Fig. 18).

A characteristic example of Nanking ware is a flagon (Plate 97) which is part of what seems to be an assemblage of several early nineteenth-century dinner services in the McCann collection bearing similar designs painted in red-orange. On the sides of the flagon, surrounding a central medallion, are four floral sprays, each of which contains a different Chinese symbol of uncertain meaning. The same symbols frequently occur in other export wares painted in underglaze colors, principally blue and red-orange, at Chingtechen.

In the flagon and in a platter of Nanking ware of the same date (Plate 98) we note the recurrence of the spear-head border in that debased version which had entered the vocabulary of the painters of Chingtechen. The platter shows a scene composed of buildings and tiny people in a rambling Chinese landscape painted in red-orange—a type of decoration repeated again and again for the Western trade during the early nineteenth century.

The orange and gold platter (Plate 99) from a McCann dinner service of about 175 pieces may be placed after 1800 during the early years of the nineteenth century. Its underglaze decoration of birds, butterflies, and flowers—all most skillfully drawn in the Chinese manner—fills every bit of the central area. The border design of grapes, leaves, and small flowers is evidently a free adaptation of a Western ceramic model. A similar design is found in Josiah Wedgwood's *First Pattern Book*, a work of the late eighteenth century; it occurs also on an example of Swansea creamware of about 1800–1810.

PLATE 96

Pierced fruit basket on a stand.
Continental market?

1790–1800

PLATE 97

Flagon of the type of porcelain known as Nanking china. American market?

BEGINNING OF THE XIX CENTURY

PLATE 98

Platter of the type of porcelain known as Nanking china. American market?

BEGINNING OF THE XIX CENTURY

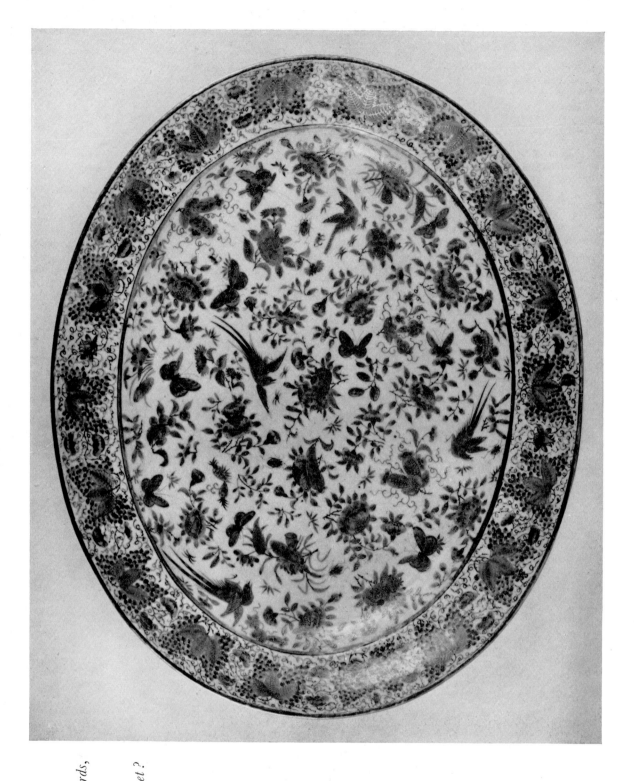

PLATE 99

Platter with a decoration of birds, butterflies, and flowers. American market?

EARLY XIX CENTURY

PORCELAINS WITH
AMERICAN EMBLEMS
1785–1820

Although the American trade in porcelain exported from China continued well into the nineteenth century, the later examples represent on the whole the routine wholesale production of Chingtechen in its least inspired moments. The best pieces produced for the American market are the earliest, and a number of these are in the McCann collection.

A typical example of the porcelain made for the American market after the historic voyage of the *Empress of China* (1784–1785) is the late eighteenth-century coffee pot (Plate 100) bearing the arms of the United States and the monogram N.E.A. within a shield. The pot has the form of a truncated cone, a shape which occurs frequently in Western ceramics. Except for the interlaced handles, one might conclude that it had been based on forms current in contemporary American silverware.

Still other examples of this late eighteenth-century style are a teapot (Plate 101) and a cup and saucer (Plate 102). The teapot is decorated with the arms of the United States; the cup and saucer with the arms of the State of New York,

a motive once popular among the citizens of that proud commonwealth.

Three other examples of porcelain made for the American market are a cup and saucer and a tea caddy (Plate 103) decorated with ships of the type engaged in the China Trade. These wares are the sort of thing that members of a crew might well have brought back with them as souvenirs of a voyage to the Far East.

A circular dish (Plate 104) with a Fitzhugh border and a central area decorated with the four Chinese symbols that frequently accompany the border was painted in the underglaze green of Chingtechen. The arms of the United States were added at Canton. Closely related to this dish is a handsome green tureen (Plate 16) with the knob described in connection with Plate 85. The painting of the tureen seems a little less precise than that of the dish, and the design of the American shield has been altered to contain a monogram M. It may be noted that a number of examples of green Fitzhugh china, possibly from several services, are in the McCann collection. A hot-water plate (Plate 105) is similar to both the pieces described above, but its underglaze decoration is in red-orange rather than in green. This piece was found not in an American collection, as might be expected, but in Macao.

PLATE 100

Coffee pot with the arms of the United States and the monogram N. E. A. American market
1795–1800

PLATE 101

Teapot with the arms of the United States and the monogram T.S. American market
1795–1800

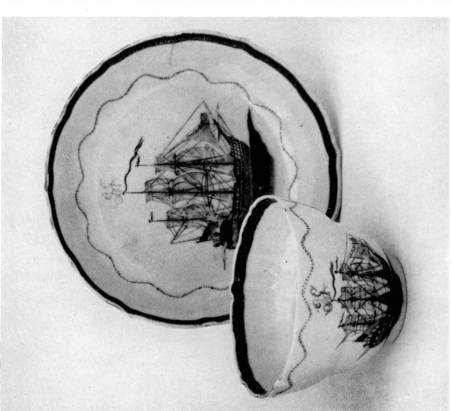

PLATE 103

Left: *Cup and saucer with ship decorations and the monogram* T. G. *American market*
Right: *Tea caddy with marine decoration. American market*

1795–1800

PLATE 104

Plate with Fitzhugh border and
the arms of the United States.
American market

EARLY XIX CENTURY

PLATE 105

Hot-water plate with Fitzhugh border and the arms of the United States. American market

EARLY XIX CENTURY

PORCELAINS MADE
FOR THE INDIAN MARKET
1785–1820

Among the McCann porcelains made for the Indian market, a large circular plate (Plate 106) is the most thoroughly Indian in decoration. The design seems to represent an opened lotus flower, with conventionalized petals radiating from the center. The central compartment contains within a square panel an inscription in Urdu, only partly legible, which begins with the words: *Vesir al-Malik*. It may be that the design was based on an Indian ceramic model. Too little, however, is known of Indian production to give definite support to such a supposition. Even the dating—from 1785 to 1800—lacks confirmation.

Two other porcelains—a platter and a tureen (Plates 107 and 108) which are evidently part of a large dinner service—have as their chief decoration an Indian rider astride an elephant, a motive used in the manner of an armorial device. The form of the tureen is similar to that of pieces made in the second half of the eighteenth century for the European market. The spear-head border, in red and gold, is debased in form, indicating a date after 1770. The two pieces could well have been made between 1785 and 1800.

A hot-water plate (Plate 109) which is similar in shape to the example bearing the United States arms (Plate 105) and of a similar date—the early nineteenth century—is decorated far differently. The ornament is in the Japanese *Imari* style; the arms, with a tiger and elephant for supporters, are patently Indian and are accompanied by an inscription in Urdu: *Vesir al-Malik Amin ad-Daur Bahadur*, which evidently refers to an Indian official.

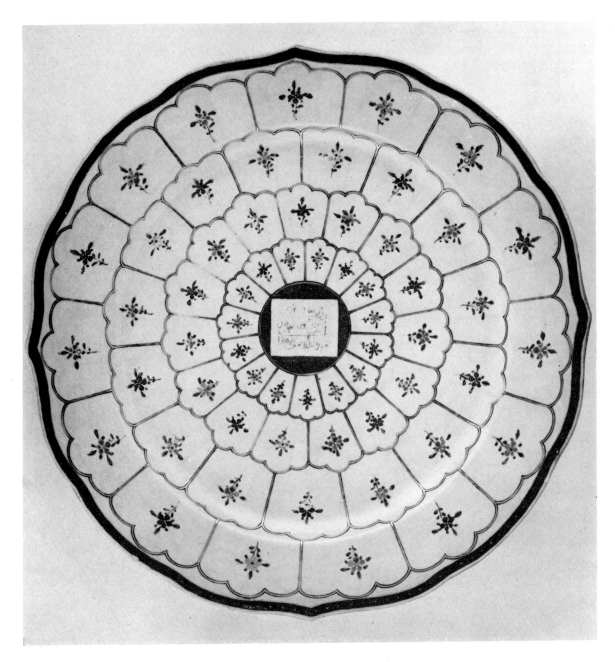

PLATE 106

Large dish with an inscription in Urdu. Indian (English colonial) market
1785–1800

PLATE 107

Platter with a mahout and elephant as a device. Indian (English colonial) market

1785–1800

PLATE 108

Tureen with a mahout and elephant as a device. Indian (English colonial) market

1785–1800

211   THE HELENA WOOLWORTH McCANN COLLECTION

PLATE 109

Hot-water plate with unidentified Indian arms and an inscription in Urdu. Indian (English colonial) market

1800–1810

APPENDIX

SELECTED BIBLIOGRAPHY

ACKNOWLEDGMENTS AND REFERENCES

INDEX

SERVICES IN THE

McCANN COLLECTION

The porcelains illustrated in Plates 1–7, 9–13, 15, 16, 18–21, 24, 28, 29, 31–33, 36–44, 46–51, 55, 56, 58, 62–64, 66–68, 71–75 (above), 76, 78–85 (above), 87, 88, 90, 92, 94–98, 101, 103, 105, 108, 109 are in The Metropolitan Museum of Art; those in Plates 8, 14, 17, 22, 23, 25–27, 30, 34, 35, 45, 52–54, 57, 59–61, 65, 69, 70, 75 (below), 77, 85 (below), 86, 89, 91, 93, 99, 100, 102, 104, 106, 107 are in the Museum of Fine Arts, Boston.

Services illustrated in the text

THE NEWTON DINNER SERVICE (Pls. 2, 21)

Examples from this service are to be found in Brooklyn, Buffalo, Chicago, Cincinnati, Cleveland, Dallas, Detroit, Freehold, Hartford, Houston, Kansas City, Los Angeles, Louisville, Minneapolis, New York, Norfolk, Omaha, Portland, Providence, Richmond, St. Louis, San Francisco, Springfield, Toledo, Toronto.

THE SEYMOUR SERVICE (Pls. 25, 26)

Examples from this service are to be found in Boston, Brooklyn, Chicago, Dallas, Detroit, Hartford, Kansas City, Los Angeles, Louisville, Minneapolis, New York, Norfolk, Providence, Springfield, Toledo, Toronto.

THE ANHALT SERVICE (Pls. 27, 28)

Examples from this service are to be found in Boston, Brooklyn, Buffalo, Chicago, Cincinnati, Dallas, Detroit, Hartford, Kansas City, Los Angeles, Louisville, Minneapolis, New York, Norfolk, Portland, Providence, Richmond, St. Louis, Springfield, Toledo, Toronto.

THE TEA SERVICE WITH AN ANTELOPE HEAD AS CREST (Pls. 31, 32)

Examples from this service are to be found in Cincinnati, Freehold, Kansas City, Minneapolis, New York, Portland, St. Louis.

THE SALDANHA SERVICE (Pls. 6, 37, 38)

Examples from this service are to be found in Boston, Brooklyn, Buffalo, Chicago, Cincinnati, Cleveland, Dallas, Detroit, Freehold, Gloucester, Hartford, Houston, Kansas City, Los Angeles, Louisville, Minneapolis, New York, Norfolk, Omaha, Portland, Providence, Richmond, St. Louis, San Francisco, Springfield, Toledo, Toronto.

THE DANISH ARMORIAL SERVICE (Pl. 39)

Examples from this service are to be found in Brooklyn, Buffalo, Chicago, Cincinnati, Cleveland, Dallas, Detroit, Freehold, Hartford, Houston, Kansas City, Los Angeles, Louisville, Minneapolis, New York, Norfolk, Omaha, Portland, Providence, Richmond, St. Louis, San Francisco, Springfield, Toledo, Toronto.

THE NEWMAN SERVICE (Pl. 44)

Examples from this service are to be found in Boston, Brooklyn, Buffalo, Chicago, Cincinnati, Cleveland, Dallas, Detroit, Freehold, Hartford, Houston, Kansas City, Los Angeles, Louisville, Minneapolis, New York, Norfolk, Omaha, Portland, Providence, Richmond, St. Louis, San Francisco, Springfield, Toledo, Toronto.

THE GRIFFITHS TEA SERVICE (Pl. 45)

Examples from this service are to be found in Boston, Brooklyn, Buffalo, Chicago, Dallas, Detroit, Hartford, Los Angeles, Louisville, Minneapolis, New York, Norfolk, Richmond, Springfield, Toledo, Toronto.

THE GORDON DINNER AND TEA SERVICES (Pls. 7, 46–48)

Examples from these services are to be found in Boston, Brooklyn, Buffalo, Chicago, Cincinnati, Cleveland, Dallas, Detroit, Freehold, Hartford, Houston, Kansas City, Los Angeles, Louisville, Minneapolis, New York, Norfolk, Omaha, Portland, Providence, Richmond, St. Louis, San Francisco, Springfield, Toledo, Toronto.

THE GRIERSON SERVICE (Pl. 49)

Examples from this service are to be found in Brooklyn, Buffalo, Chicago, Cincinnati, Cleveland, Dallas, Detroit, Freehold, Hartford, Houston, Kansas City, Los Angeles, Louisville, Minneapolis, New York, Norfolk, Omaha, Portland, Providence, Richmond, St. Louis, San Francisco, Springfield, Toledo.

THE DINNER SERVICE WITH FRENCH (?) ARMS (Pl. 51)

Examples from this service are to be found in Boston, Brooklyn, Buffalo, Chicago, Cincinnati, Cleveland, Dallas, Detroit, Freehold, Hartford, Houston, Kansas City, Los Angeles, Louisville, Minneapolis, New York, Norfolk, Omaha, Portland, Providence, Richmond, St. Louis, San Francisco, Springfield, Toledo, Toronto.

THE DINNER SERVICE WITH A HUNTING SCENE (Pl. 10)

Examples from this service are to be found in Cincinnati, Houston, Kansas City, Minneapolis, New York, Omaha, Portland, St. Louis, San Francisco, Toronto.

THE TEA SERVICE WITH VENUS AND MERCURY (Pl. 66, above)

Examples from this service are to be found in Brooklyn, Chicago, Los Angeles, Minneapolis, New York, Omaha, Portland.

THE DINNER SERVICE WITH FRUIT DECORATION (Pl. 68)

Examples from this service are to be found in Brooklyn, Buffalo, Chicago, Cincinnati, Cleveland, Dallas, Detroit, Freehold, Hartford, Houston, Kansas City, Los Angeles, Louisville, Minneapolis, New York, Norfolk, Portland, Providence, Richmond, St. Louis, Springfield, Toledo.

THE HAMMOND SERVICE (Pls. 14, 79)

Examples from this service are to be found in Boston, Brooklyn, Buffalo, Chicago, Cincinnati, Cleveland, Hartford, Houston, Kansas City, Minneapolis, New York, Omaha, Portland, Richmond, St. Louis, San Francisco, Springfield, Toronto.

THE ARAUJO DE ACEBEDO SERVICE (Pl. 80)

Examples from this service are to be found in Boston, Brooklyn, Buffalo, Chicago, Cincinnati, Cleveland, Dallas, Detroit, Freehold, Hartford, Houston, Kansas City, Los Angeles, Louisville, Minneapolis, New York, Norfolk, Omaha, Portland, Providence, Richmond, St. Louis, San Francisco, Springfield, Toledo, Toronto.

THE SILVEIRA SERVICE (Pls. 15, 81, 82)

Examples from this service are to be found in Boston, Brooklyn, Buffalo, Chicago, Cincinnati, Cleveland, Dallas, Detroit, Freehold, Houston, Kansas City, Los Angeles, Louisville, Minneapolis, New York, Norfolk, Omaha, Portland, Providence, Richmond, St. Louis, San Francisco, Springfield, Toledo.

THE G.P.C. SERVICE (Pl. 85, above)

Examples from this service are to be found in Boston, Brooklyn, Buffalo, Chicago, Cincinnati, Cleveland, Dallas, Detroit, Hartford, Houston, Kansas City, Los Angeles, Louisville, Minneapolis, New York, Norfolk, Omaha, Portland, Providence, Richmond, St. Louis, San Francisco, Springfield, Toledo.

THE J.A. SERVICE (Pl. 85, below)

Examples from this service are to be found in Boston, Brooklyn, Buffalo, Chicago, Dallas, Detroit, Hartford, Kansas City, Los Angeles, Louisville, Minneapolis, Norfolk, Providence, Richmond, Springfield, Toledo.

THE CORNUCOPIA SERVICE (Pls. 94, 95)

Examples from this service are to be found in Boston, Brooklyn, Buffalo, Chicago, Dallas, Detroit, Hartford, Kansas City, Los Angeles, Louisville, Minneapolis, New York, Norfolk, Portland, Providence, Richmond, Springfield, Toledo, Toronto.

ORANGE FITZHUGH SERVICES (Pl. 97)

Examples from these services are to be found in Boston, Brooklyn, Buffalo, Chicago, Cincinnati, Cleveland, Dallas, Detroit, Freehold, Hartford, Houston, Kansas City, Los Angeles, Louisville, Minneapolis, New York, Norfolk, Omaha, Portland, Providence, Richmond, San Francisco, St. Louis, Springfield, Toledo.

THE SERVICE DECORATED WITH BIRDS, BUTTER-FLIES, AND FLOWERS (Pl. 99)

Examples from this service are to be found in Boston, Brooklyn, Buffalo, Chicago, Dallas, Detroit, Hartford, Los Angeles, Louisville, Minneapolis, New York, Norfolk, Richmond, Springfield, Toledo.

GREEN FITZHUGH PORCELAINS (Pl. 104)

Examples from various sets decorated with the Fitzhugh borders are to be found in Brooklyn, Buffalo, Chicago, Cincinnati, Detroit, Kansas City, Los Angeles, Minneapolis, New York, Norfolk, Richmond, St. Louis, Springfield, Toledo.

Other services in the McCann collection

THE J.V.P. DINNER SERVICE

Gold and blue borders. Initial within oval medallion. A plate in the group not only has identical border patterns but bears the Hammond arms, exactly as they appear on one of the plates in the Hammond service. Made for the English market. 1785–1800. The Metropolitan Museum of Art

Examples from this service are to be found in Brooklyn, Buffalo, Chicago, Cincinnati, Cleveland, Dallas, Detroit, Freehold, Hartford, Houston, Kansas City, Los Angeles, Louisville, Minneapolis, New York, Norfolk, Omaha, Portland, Providence, Richmond, St. Louis, San Francisco, Springfield, Toledo.

THE SERVICE WITH ORANGE AND SEPIA BORDERS

Similar in type of design to the J. V. P. service. Within the oval medallions were the initials T. L. C. A. R. B., now erased from most of the pieces in the service. Probably English market. 1785–1800. The Metropolitan Museum of Art

Examples from this service are to be found in Boston, Brooklyn, Buffalo, Chicago, Cincinnati, Cleveland, Dallas, Detroit, Freehold, Hartford, Houston, Kansas City, Los Angeles, Louisville, Minneapolis, New York, Norfolk, Omaha, Portland, Providence, Richmond, St. Louis, San Francisco, Springfield, Toledo, Toronto.

THE DINNER SERVICE WITH WIDE BLUE AND GOLD BORDERS

Repeats of flowering sprays separated by four compartments enclosing diamond-shaped motives form the borders. European market. 1785–1800. The Metropolitan Museum of Art

Examples from this service are to be found in Boston, Brooklyn, Buffalo, Chicago, Cincinnati, Cleveland, Dallas, Detroit, Freehold, Hartford, Houston, Kansas City, Los Angeles, Louisville, Minneapolis, New York, Norfolk, Omaha, Portland, Providence, Richmond, St. Louis, San Francisco, Springfield, Toledo.

THE TEA SERVICE WITH THE MONOGRAM C

Decorated at the rim with a zigzag ribbon pattern in blue and gold. The mantling of the spade-shaped shield is characteristic of late eighteenth-century armorial decoration. English market. 1790–1800. The Metropolitan Museum of Art

Examples from this service are to be found in Brooklyn, Chicago, Cleveland, Detroit, Freehold, Los Angeles, New York, Portland, Toledo.

A MINIATURE TEA SERVICE WITH THE INITIALS M. M.

Narrow borders in salmon, blue, and gold. Initials within spade-shaped shield. Mantling similar to that of foregoing service. English market. 1790–1800. The Metropolitan Museum of Art

Examples from this service are to be found in Brooklyn, Cincinnati, Cleveland, Kansas City, Minneapolis, New York, Omaha, Portland, St. Louis.

THE E. A. C. DINNER SERVICE

Narrow borders, painted with a grape pattern in gold on blue (see Plate 99). Initials within oval medallion. Probably made for the English market. 1790–1800. The Metropolitan Museum of Art

Examples from this service are to be found in Brooklyn, Buffalo, Chicago, Cincinnati, Cleveland, Dallas, Detroit, Freehold, Hartford, Houston, Kansas City, Los Angeles, Louisville, Minneapolis, New York, Norfolk, Portland, Providence, Richmond, St. Louis, Springfield, Toledo.

THE T. H. A. B. DINNER SERVICE

Grape border in sepia and gold (see Plate 99). Initials within a spade-shaped shield surmounted by a crest. English market. 1790–1800. The Metropolitan Museum of Art

Examples from this service are to be found in Boston, Brooklyn, Buffalo, Chicago, Dallas, Detroit, Hartford, Kansas City, Los Angeles, Louisville, Minneapolis, New York, Norfolk, Providence, Richmond, Springfield, Toledo, Toronto.

SERVICES DECORATED IN UNDERGLAZE BLUE
WITH FITZHUGH BORDERS OR RELATED
MOTIVES

Made for American and European markets. Chiefly
early nineteenth century. The Metropolitan Museum
of Art

Examples from these services are to be found in
Boston, Brooklyn, Buffalo, Chicago, Cincinnati, Cleve-
land, Dallas, Detroit, Freehold, Hartford, Houston,
Kansas City, Los Angeles, Louisville, Minneapolis,
New York, Norfolk, Omaha, Portland, Providence,
Richmond, St. Louis, San Francisco, Springfield,
Toledo, Toronto.

THE DINNER SERVICE WITH THE INITIALS T. J.

Decorated in underglaze blue with Fitzhugh border.
In center: ships. Made for the English market. Early
nineteenth century. The Metropolitan Museum of Art
Examples from this service are to be found in Boston,
Brooklyn, Buffalo, Chicago, Dallas, Detroit, Hartford,
Kansas City, Los Angeles, Louisville, Minneapolis,
New York, Norfolk, Providence, Richmond, Spring-
field.

Belevitch-Stankevitch, H. *Le Goût chinois en France au temps de Louis XIV*. Paris (Jean Schemit), 1910

A basic work on the development of the taste for things Chinese which culminated in the chinoiserie style

Boxer, C. R. *Fidalgos in the Far East, 1550–1770: Fact and Fancy in the History of Macao*. The Hague (Martinus Nijhoff), 1948

A history of the Portuguese settlement at Macao, of the trade there, and of the customs of the people

Brankston, A. D. *Early Ming Wares of Chingtechen*. Peking (Henry Vetch), 1938

An important contribution to the studies of the porcelains of Chingtechen

Burton, William, F.C.S. *Porcelain: a Sketch of Its Nature, Art and Manufacture*. London (Cassell & Co., Ltd.), 1906

Contains translations into English of the major portions of Father d'Entrecolles's letters

Bushell, Stephen W[ootton]. *Description of Chinese Pottery and Porcelain: Being a Translation of the* T'ao Shuo. Oxford (Clarendon Press), 1910

The *T'ao Shuo* and the *Ching-tê-chên T'ao Lu* (the latter translated by G. R. Sayer) are basic works for the study of Chinese porcelain

————. *Oriental Ceramic Art*. New York (D. Appleton and Co.), 1899

A standard history of Chinese porcelain

Chang, T'ien-Tsê. *Sino-Portuguese Trade from 1514 to 1644: a Synthesis of Portuguese and Chinese Sources*. Leyden (Late E. J. Brill, Ltd.), 1934

Contains descriptions of the trade in Canton prior to the arrival of the Portuguese, as well as an account of Portuguese activities there

Crisp, Frederick Arthur. *Armorial China: a Catalogue of Chinese Porcelain with Coats of Arms*. Privately printed, 1907

Dillon, Edward. *Porcelain*. New York (G. P. Putnam's Sons), 1904

Contains a chapter tracing the growth of knowledge of and appreciation for porcelain in the West

Du Halde, J. B., s.j. *Description géographique, historique, chronologique et physique de l'empire de la Chine et de la Tartarre chinoise*. 4 vols. Paris, 1735

A description of China at the beginning of the age of the China Trade

————. *A Description of the Empire of China . . .* 2 vols. London, 1738

Translation into English of the *Description . . . de la Chine*

English Ceramic Circle. *English Pottery and Porcelain: Commemorative Catalogue of an Exhibition Held at the Victoria and Albert Museum, May 5th—June 20th, 1948*. London (Routledge and Kegan Paul, Ltd.), 1949

Espirito Santo Silva, Ricardo R., and Hyde, J. A. Lloyd. *Chinese Porcelains for the European Market*. Lisbon (Bertrand Lda). In press

Includes many plates in color after paintings by Eduardo Malta

Foster, Sir William. *England's Quest of Eastern Trade*. London (A. & C. Black, Ltd.), 1933

Goidsenhoven, J. P. van. *La Céramique chinoise sous les Ts'ing, 1644–1851*. Brussels, 1936

Contains descriptions and illustrations of a number of examples of China-Trade porcelain

Hernmarck, Carl. *Marieberg: en Lysande Representant för Svenskt Sjuttonhundratal*. Stockholm (Wahlström and Widstrand), 1946

Hibbert, Eloise Talcott. *Jesuit Adventure in China during the Reign of K'ang Hsi*. New York (E. P. Dutton & Co.), 1941

Hickey, William. *Memoirs of William Hickey*. Edited by Alfred Spencer. London (Hurst & Blackett, Ltd.), 1913

Contains a description of Canton by the author, who visited there in 1769

Hobson, R. L. *Chinese Pottery and Porcelain: an Account of the Potter's Art in China from Primitive Times to the Present Day*. Vol. II (Ming and Ch'ing Porcelain). London (Cassell & Co., Ltd.), 1915

Honey, William Bowyer. *The Ceramic Art of China and Other Countries of the Far East*. London (Faber & Faber, Ltd., and The Hyperion Press, Ltd.), 1945

————. *Dresden China*. London (A. & C. Black, Ltd.), 1934

————. *European Ceramic Art: a Dictionary of Factories, Artists, Technical Terms, Et Cetera*. London (Faber & Faber, Ltd.), 1952

Hudson, G. F. *Europe and China: a Survey of Their Relations from the Earliest Times to 1800*. London (Edward Arnold & Co.), 1931

Huxley, Gervas. *Tea in Porcelain: a Study of English Tea Drinking and English Porcelain Tea Ware, 1750–1800*. London (The Tea Centre), 1952

Hyde, J. A. Lloyd. *Oriental Lowestoft, Chinese Export Porcelain, Porcelaine de la Cie des Indes*. Newport, Monmouthshire (The Ceramic Book Company), 1954

A reprint of Hyde's *Oriental Lowestoft*, New York (Harper & Bros.), 1936, with the addition of illustrations in color

————, and Espirito Santo Silva, Ricardo R. *Chinese Porcelains for the European Market*. Lisbon (Bertrand Lda). In press

Includes many plates in color after paintings by Eduardo Malta

Ibn Battúta (Muhammed ibn 'Abd Allāh). *Travels in Asia and Africa, 1325–1354*. Translated and selected by H. A. R. Gibb. New York (Robert M. McBride & Co.), 1929

Contains a brief description of Canton (Sín-Kalán)

Jenyns, Soame. *Later Chinese Porcelain: the Ch'ing Dynasty (1644–1912)*. London (Faber & Faber, Ltd.), 1951

The most recent and best description of Chinese porcelain of the age of the China Trade

Jourdain, Margaret, and Jenyns, R. Soame. *Chinese Export Art in the Eighteenth Century*. London (Country Life, Ltd.) and New York (Charles Scribner's Sons), 1950

Contains a chapter on porcelain made for export to the West

Kimball, Fiske. *The Creation of the Rococo*. Philadelphia (Philadelphia Museum of Art), 1943

Lawrence, Amos A. Catalogue of the sale of his collection held at the American Art Galleries, New York, March 29—April 2, 1921

An extensive collection of China-Trade porcelains, many of which are illustrated

Lenz, Frank B. "The World's Ancient Porcelain Center." *The National Geographic Magazine*, XXXVIII (November, 1920), pp. 391–406

A description of Chingtechen by the author, who visited there in 1920

Los Angeles County Museum. "American Ships in the China Trade." *Bulletin of the Art Division*, VII (Winter, 1955), no. 1. Catalogue of a loan exhibition

A succinct account of the China Trade, especially as concerns trade to the United States

Mankowitz, Wolf. *Wedgwood*. London (B. T. Batsford, Ltd.), 1953

Metropolitan Museum of Art. *The China Trade and Its Influence*. New York, 1941

A handbook of an exhibition held at the Metropolitan Museum, including articles on aspects of the subject by Margaret E. Scherer and Joseph Downs, a bibliography, and numerous illustrations

Monkhouse, Cosmo. *A History and Description of Chinese Porcelain*. London (Cassell & Co., Ltd.), 1901

Morison, Samuel Eliot. *The Maritime History of Massachusetts*. Boston and New York (Houghton, Mifflin Co.), 1921

Contains an account of the beginnings of trade between the United States and the Far East

Morse, Hosea Ballou. *The Chronicles of the East India Company Trading to China, 1635–1834*. Cambridge (Harvard University Press) and Oxford (The Clarendon Press), 1926 (Vols. 1–4); 1929 (Vol. 5)

A study of the foreign trade at Canton based on Company documents

————. *The Gilds of China*. London (Longmans, Green, & Co.), 1909

————. *The International Relations of the Chinese Empire*. London (Longmans, Green, & Co.), 1910

Contains a summary of the commercial relations between East and West in the eighteenth century, and a description of the political and economic systems of China

Reichwein, Adolf. *China and Europe: Intellectual and Artistic Contacts in the Eighteenth Century*. New York (Alfred A. Knopf), 1925

Riesebieter, O. *Die deutschen Fayencen des 17. und 18. Jahrhunderts*. Leipzig (Klinkhardt and Biermann), 1921

Rowbotham, Arnold H. *Missionary and Mandarin: the Jesuits at the Court of China*. Berkeley and Los Angeles (University of California Press), 1942

Sayer, Geoffrey R. *Ching-tê-chên T'ao Lu, or The Potteries of China: . . . a Translation with Notes and an Introduction.* London (Routledge and Kegan Paul, Ltd.), 1951
The *Ching-tê-chên T'ao Lu* is one of the basic books for the study of Chinese porcelains.

Schmidt, Robert. *Porcelain as an Art and a Mirror of Fashion.* Translated and edited with an Introduction by W. A. Thorpe. London (George G. Harrap & Co., Ltd.), 1932
A social and historical study of European porcelain

Shaw, Major Samuel. *The Journals of Major Samuel Shaw, with a Life of the Author by Josiah Quincy.* Boston (Wm. Crosby & H. P. Nichols), 1847

Sirén, Osvald. *China and Gardens of Europe of the Eighteenth Century.* New York (The Ronald Press Co.), 1950

Staunton, Sir George. *An Authentic Account of an Embassy from the King of Great Britain to the Emperor of China . . .* London (printed by W. Bulmer & Co. for G. Nicol), 1797
The author visited China as a member of the Macartney Embassy.

Tudor-Craig, Sir Algernon. *Armorial Porcelain of the Eighteenth Century.* London (The Century House), 1925
A basic work in the study of China-Trade porcelain

Williamson, G. C. *The Book of Famille Rose.* London (Methuen & Co.), 1927
A description of this famous eighteenth-century variety of Chinese porcelain

Yamada, Chisaburo. *Die Chinamode des Spätbarock.* Berlin (Würfel Verlag), 1935
Deals with the impact of China on European art

Zimmermann, Ernst. *Meissner Porzellan.* Leipzig (Verlag Karl W. Hiersemann), 1926

ACKNOWLEDGMENTS AND REFERENCES

Quotations and illustrations in the text are acknowledged below

PAGE

2. "The sight . . . flames." Tr. Bushell, *Oriental Ceramic Art*, p. 284

2 f. "Ten thousand *li* . . . me." Quoted by Brankston, p. 39

4. Figure 2. Photograph by Frank B. Lenz. After *The National Geographic Magazine*, XXXVIII (November, 1920), p. 393

4. Nanchang "has always . . . Magistrates." Du Halde, I, p. 80

5. "*King-te-ching* . . . Robbers." Quoted by Du Halde, I, pp. 80 f.

5. "dotted . . . describe." Lenz, p. 397

6. "it seems . . . Materials." Du Halde, I, p. 80

6. boats "come . . . bricks." Quoted by Burton, p. 86

7. "so steep . . . stairs." Du Halde, I, p. 83

7. Figure 3. Photograph by John R. Freeman & Co.

8. "In a Place . . . Task." Quoted by Du Halde, I, pp. 341 f.

8 f. Figures 4, 5, 6. Photographs by A. D. Brankston. Reproduced from his *Early Ming Wares of Ching-techen*, Peking (Henry Vetch), 1938, pls. 36 (above), 37, and 36 (below) respectively

8 f. D'Entrecolles's description of porcelain manufacture. Du Halde, I, p. 342

9. "it is surprising . . . self." Quoted by Du Halde, I, p. 342

9. "the manufacture . . . alike." Quoted by Bushell, *Oriental Ceramic Art*, p. 430

9. "To hasten . . . make." Quoted by Du Halde, I, p. 343

9. "the Painting . . . all." Quoted by Du Halde, I, p. 343

PAGE

10. "during . . . artistry." Quoted by Brankston, p. 19

12 ff. "the view . . . Danes." Hickey, pp. 198, 201 f.

14. "The handsome . . . strangers." Staunton, pp. 365 ff.

14. "the limits . . . view." Shaw, pp. 178 f.

15. Figure 9. Photograph by Country Life Ltd. for Jourdain and Jenyns, *Chinese Export Art in the Eighteenth Century*, London (Country Life Ltd.), 1950, fig. 2

15. Canton's favored geographical position. Chang, p. 4

16. Canton's Moslem colony in the fourteenth century. Ibn Battúta, p. 290

16. "within . . . post-roads." Chang, pp. 27 f.

16. " a man . . . meat." Chang, pp. 27 f.

16 f. "gold . . . etc." Chang, p. 20

17. "also . . . Cathay." Chang, pp. 36 f.

17. "they . . . gain." Chang, p. 36

17. Figure 10. Courtesy of the Peabody Museum of Salem

19. Figure 12. Victoria and Albert Museum, London. Crown copyright

21. "The people . . . land." Chang, pp. 116 f.

22. "for the honour . . . therabouts." Foster, p. 146

22. "Concerning . . . have." Morse, *Chronicles*, I, p. 29

28. "9·85 taels . . . duccatoons." Morse, *Chronicles*, I, p. 69

28. "not simply . . . honesty." Morse, *Chronicles*, I, pp. 66 f.

29. "It was . . . people." Shaw, pp. 128 f.

30. Figure 18. Courtesy of the Henry Francis duPont Winterthur Museum, Winterthur, Delaware

PAGE

31. "In view . . . all!" Morison, p. 76

31. Figure 19. Photograph by George M. Cushing, Jr.

32. "that the English . . . America." Morse, *Chronicles*, II, p. 253

33. "The best commentary . . . traders." Morse, *The Gilds of China*, p. 80

33. "As the Requests . . . Intentions." Morse, *Chronicles*, II, p. 251

35. "Chinaware . . . all." Morse, *Chronicles*, I, p. 164

35. "one 'having Judgment . . . respect'." Morse, *Chronicles*, I, pp. 220 f.

36. Figure 22, below. Victoria and Albert Museum, London. Crown copyright

36. "we find . . . Good." Morse, *Chronicles*, V, p. 43

36. "which being done . . . Merchandise." Morse, *Chronicles*, V, pp. 43 f.

37. Figure 23. Photograph by Country Life Ltd. for Jourdain and Jenyns, *Chinese Export Art in the Eighteenth Century*, London (Country Life Ltd.), 1950, fig. 10

37. "We were . . . years." Hickey, p. 209

37. "Tho' the number . . . Province." Du Halde, I, p. 114

37. "very industrious . . . Perfection." Du Halde, I, p. 114

37. "Copy . . . copy." Williamson, p. 121

37 f. "In my possession . . . successful." Monkhouse, p. 139

38. "are not much esteem'd . . . slight." Du Halde, I, p. 114

38 f. "[Potts] . . . warehouse." Quoted by Hyde, p. 16

38 f. Figures 25, 26. Photographs by John R. Freeman & Co.

42. "Great value . . . custom." Belevitch-Stankevitch, pp. xxxiii f.

43. "*Allons . . . Chine.*" Quoted by Belevitch-Stankevitch, p. 150

45. "I almost think . . . theology." Quoted by Reichwein, p. 80

46. "China . . . Heaven." Quoted by Hudson, p. 318

46. Figure 29. Courtesy of the British Travel and Holidays Association

48. Figure 30. Copyrighted and all rights reserved by the Albertina, Vienna

49. Figure 31. Photograph by K. Gundermann in The Metropolitan Museum of Art

PAGE

53. "that the Dutch . . . [of England]." Quoted by Goidsenhoven, p. 251

53. Figure 33. Reproduced from J. P. van Goidsenhoven, *La Céramique chinoise sous les Ts'ing*, Brussels, 1936, pl. 110, nos. 260, 261

56. Figure 35. Reproduced from Egerton Castle, *English Book-Plates*, London (George Bell & Sons), 1892

57. "From the debris . . . ago." Quoted by Hobson, II, pp. 252 f.

57. Figure 36. Drawing by Lucina Wakefield

58. Figure 37. Drawing by Lucina Wakefield. Chinese motives adapted from S. Jenyns, *Later Chinese Porcelain: the Ch'ing Dynasty (1644–1912)*, London (Faber & Faber Ltd.), 1951, pls. LXXVIII and LXIII, respectively

58. Figure 38. Drawing by Lucina Wakefield

60. Earliest use of rose-pink color. Honey, *The Ceramic Art of China*, p. 151

60. "The rose-pink . . . derived." Honey, *The Ceramic Art of China*, p. 151

60. Rose enamels first made at *Ku-li*. Sayer, p. 72

65. Figure 39. Courtesy of the Museum of Fine Arts, Boston

92. Armorial platter . . . made for Robert Bigland. Tudor-Craig, *Armorial Porcelain*

110. Meissen plate of about 1760. Illustrated in Zimmermann's *Meissner Porzellan*, p. 246, Abb. 89

116. Figure 41. After O. Riesebieter, *Die deutschen Fayencen, des 17. und 18. Jahrhunderts*. Leipzig (Klinkhardt and Biermann), 1921, fig. 50

124. Figure 42. Photograph by Franklin A. Barrett for his *Worcester Porcelain*, London (Faber & Faber Ltd.), 1953, pl. 32 A

134. Figure 43. Detail from a photograph by A. Dingjan. The same piece is illustrated by C. H. de Jonge, "Dodici piatti di ceramica di Delft," *Faenza*, XXXIX (1953), pl. XLV

137. Figure 44. Reproduced from J. P. van Goidsenhoven, *La Céramique chinoise sous les Ts'ing*, Brussels, 1936, pl. 117

147. Figure 46, above. Copyrighted by the Cecil Higgins Trustees. Photograph by Fine Arts Engravers Ltd., London

150. Figure 47. Copyright British Museum

152. Figure 48. Reproduced from the English Ceramic Circle, *Transactions*, II, no. 8, 1942, pl. 51 b

PAGE

162. Figures 52, 53. Copyright Nationalmuseum, Stockholm

180. Figure 56. Reproduced from Wolf Mankowitz, *Wedgwood*, London (B. T. Batsford, Ltd.), 1953, pl. 2, no. 4

184. Jourdain and Jenyns. *Chinese Export Art*, pp. 120 f., figs. 94, 96. Figure 94 shows the digits "79" possibly signifying the date 1779.

188. Figure 57. Reproduced from A. Dayot, *La Révolution française*, Paris (Ernest Flammarion), n. d., p. 234

PAGE

192. New Hall mug. Illustrated in the English Ceramic Circle's *English Pottery and Porcelain*, pl. 119, no. 541

192. Handles used at the Criseby and Eckernförde pottery works. Illustrated in Riesebieter's *Die deutschen Fayencen des 17. und 18. Jahrhunderts*, p. 271, Abb. 316

196. Wedgwood's *First Pattern Book*. Mankowitz, *Wedgwood*, pl. v, no. 79 (facing p. 58)

196. Swansea creamware. E. M. Nance, *The Pottery and Porcelain of Swansea and Nantgarw*, London, 1942, pl. VIII, E (facing p. 39)

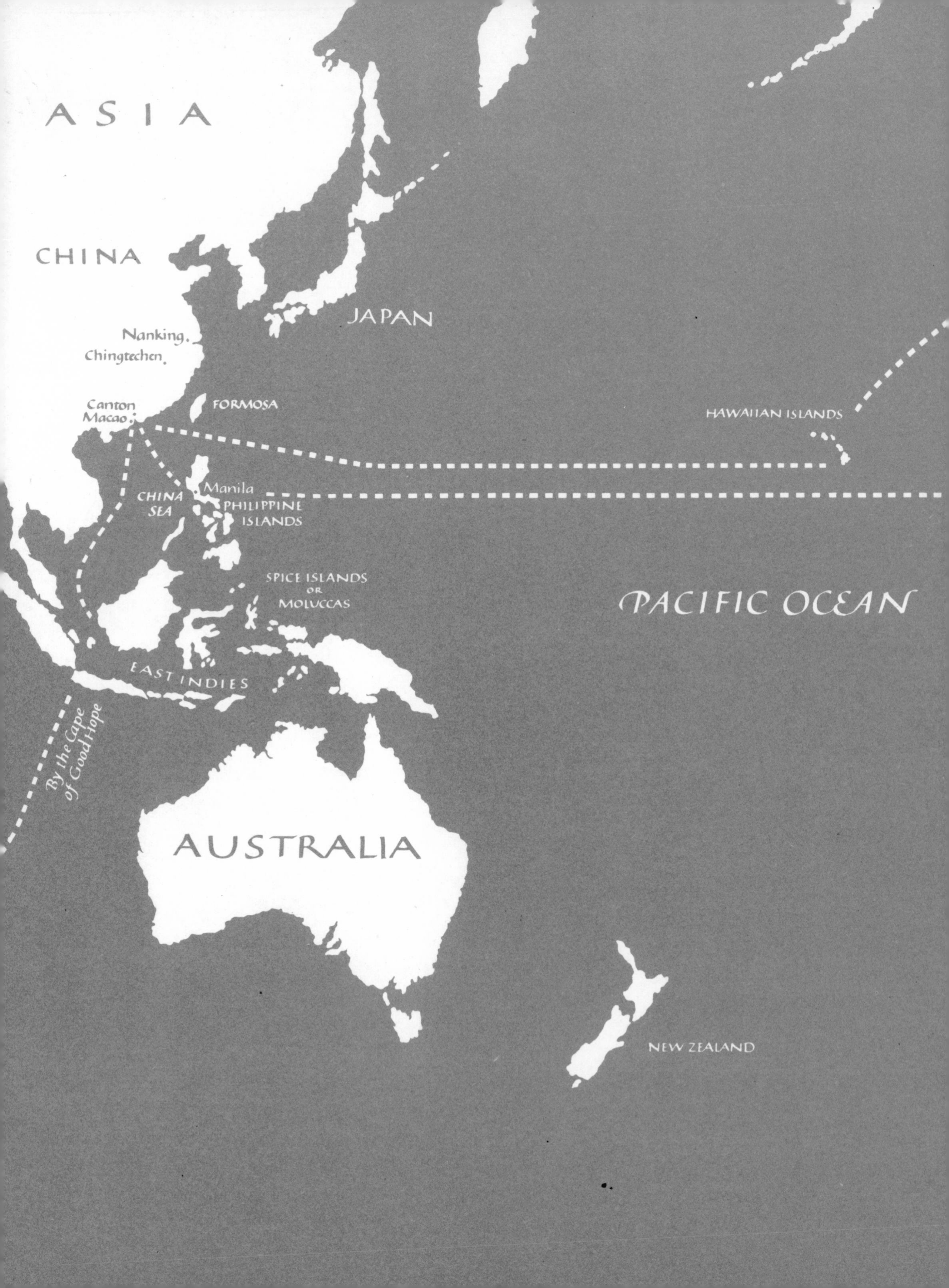
ASIA
CHINA
JAPAN
Nanking
Chingtechen
Canton
Macao
FORMOSA
HAWAIIAN ISLANDS
Manila
CHINA SEA
PHILIPPINE ISLANDS
SPICE ISLANDS OR MOLUCCAS
PACIFIC OCEAN
EAST INDIES
By the Cape of Good Hope
AUSTRALIA
NEW ZEALAND